Lecture Notes in Computer Science 8435

Commenced Publication in 1973
Founding and Former Series Editors:
Gerhard Goos, Juris Hartmanis, and Jan van Leeuwen

T0212698

Axel Sikora   Marion Berbineau
Alexey Vinel   Magnus Jonsson
Alain Pirovano   Marina Aguado (Eds.)

Communication Technologies for Vehicles

6th International Workshop
Nets4Cars/Nets4Trains/Nets4Aircraft 2014
Offenburg, Germany, May 6-7, 2014
Proceedings

Springer

Volume Editors

Axel Sikora
Offenburg University of Applied Sciences, Offenburg, Germany
E-mail: axel.sikora@hs-offenburg.de

Marion Berbineau
IFSTTAR, Villeneuve d'Ascq, France
E-mail: marion.berbineau@ifsttar.fr

Alexey Vinel
Tampere University of Technology, Tampere, Finland
E-mail: alexey.vinel@tut.fi

Magnus Jonsson
Halmstad University, Halmstad, Sweden
E-mail: magnus.jonsson@ide.hh.se

Alain Pirovano
Ecole Nationale de l'Aviation, Toulouse, France
E-mail: alain.pirovano@enac.fr

Marina Aguado
University of the Basque Country, Bilbao, Spain
E-mail: marina.aguado@ehu.es

ISSN 0302-9743   e-ISSN 1611-3349
ISBN 978-3-319-06643-1   e-ISBN 978-3-319-06644-8
DOI 10.1007/978-3-319-06644-8
Springer Cham Heidelberg New York Dordrecht London

Library of Congress Control Number: 2014936858

LNCS Sublibrary: SL 5 – Computer Communication Networks and
Telecommunications

Typesetting: Camera-ready by author, data conversion by Scientific Publishing Services, Chennai, India

Printed on acid-free paper

Springer is part of Springer Science+Business Media (www.springer.com)

Preface

The Communication Technologies for Vehicles Workshop series provides an international forum on the latest technologies and research in the field of intra- and inter-vehicles communications and is organized annually to present original research results in all areas related to physical layer, communication protocols and standards, mobility and traffic models, experimental and field operational testing, and performance analysis.

First launched by Tsutomu Tsuboi, Alexey Vinel, and Fei Liu in Saint Petersburg, Russia (2009), Nets4Cars workshops have been held in Newcastle-upon-Tyne, UK (2010), Oberpfaffenhofen, Germany (2011), Vilnius, Lithuania (2012) and Villeneuve d'Ascq, France (2013). These proceedings contain the papers presented at the 6th International Workshop on Communication Technologies for Vehicles (Nets4Cars- Nets4Trains-Nets4Aircraft 2014), which took place at Offenburg University of Applied Sciences, Germany, in May 2014, with the technical support of IFSTTAR, France, and Halmstad University, Sweden. The sponsor of the event was Alcatel - Lucent Stiftung für Kommunikationsforschung.

Our call for papers resulted in 15 submissions. Each of them was assigned to the Technical Program Committee members and 10 submissions were accepted for publication. Each accepted paper got at least two independent reviews. In addition, four invited papers were accepted. The order of the papers in these proceedings corresponds to the workshop program.

This year the keynote speakers were:

- Hans-Peter Mayer "Car Specific Services in 5G Frameworks," Lead Next Generation Wireless, Bell Labs, Stuttgart, Germany
- Thomas Hogenmüller "Overview and Challenges of Automotive E/E-Architecture with Ethernet," Team Manager E/E-Architectures Communication Technologies and Gateways, R. Bosch GmbH, Stuttgart, Germany
- Torsten Braun "Routing Protocols for and Deployment of Flying Ad-hoc Networks," Professor of Computer Science, University of Bern, Switzerland
- Marion Berbineau "Wireless Communications for Railway Applications: State of Knowledge and Future Trends," Research Director, Deputy Manager COSYS Department (COmponents and SYStems), IFSTTAR, France

We extend a sincere "thank you" to all the authors who submitted the results of their recent work, to all the members of our hard-working comprehensive Technical Program Committee, as well as the thoughtful external reviewers.

Also, we extend a special "thank you" to Nikita Lyamin for the preparation of the proceedings and Bertram Birk for managing the website.

We invite all the experts in the field to join us in St. Petersburg, Russia, for Nets4Cars-Fall in October 2014.

May 2014

Axel Sikora
Marion Berbineau
Alexey Vinel
Magnus Jonsson
Alain Pirovano
Marina Aguado

Organization

Nets4Cars 2014 was organized by Offenburg University of Applied Sciences, Offenburg, Germany.

Executive Committee

General Co-chairs

Axel Sikora	HS Offenburg, Germany
Marion Berbineau	IFSTTAR, France
Alexey Vinel	TUT, Finland

TPC Co-chairs

Magnus Jonsson	HH, Sweden
Alain Pirovano	ENAC, France
Marina Aguado	UPV/EHU, Spain

Web Chair

Bertram Birk	HS Offenburg, Germany

Publication Chair

Nikita Lyamin	HH, Sweden

Steering Committee

Marion Berbineau	IFSTTAR, France
Xu Li	State University of New York, USA
Antonella Molinaro	University of Calabria Region, Italy
Joel Rodrigues	University of Beira Interior, Portugal
Tsutomu Tsuboi	Hamamatsu Agency for Innovation, Japan
Axel Sikora	HS Offenburg, Germany
Thomas Strang	DLR, Germany
Alexey Vinel	Tampere University of Technology, Finland
Yan Zhang	Simula Research Lab and University of Oslo, Norway

Technical Program Committee

Onur Altintas	Toyota InfoTechnology Center, Japan
Petros Belimpasakis	Bang & Olufsen, Germany
Erwin Biebl	Technische Universität München, Germany
Hervé Boeglen	Laboratoire XLIM-SIC, France
Mohamed Boucadair	France Telecom, France
Torsten Braun	University of Bern, Switzerland
Teodor Buburuzan	Volkswagen Group Research, Germany
Marcello Caleffi	UNINA, Italy
Claudia Campolo	University Mediterranea of Reggio Calabria, Italy
Eduardo Cerqueira	UFPA, Brazil
Marilia Curado	University of Coimbra, Portugal
Robil Daher	German University in Cairo, Egypt
Thierry Delot	University of Lille North of France, France
Konrad Doll	HS Aschaffenburg, Germany
Dhavy Gantsou	UVHC, France
Benoit Geller	ENSTA Paris Tech, France
Javier Goikoetxea	CAF, Spain
Javier Gozalvez	UMH, Spain
Geert Heijenk	University of Twente, The Netherlands
Benoit Hilt	University of Haute Alsace, France
Muhammad Ali Imran	University of Surrey, UK
Uwe Kucharzyk	Bombardier Transportation, Germany
Anis Laouiti	TELECOM SudParis, France
Andreas Lehner	DLR, Germany
Katrin Lüddecke	DLR, Germany
Juliette Marais	IFSTTAR, France
Francesca Martelli	IIT - CNR, Italy
Michael Meyer zu Hoerste	DLR, Germany
Brian Park	University of Virginia, USA
Paolo Santi	IIT-CNR, Italy
Vasco Soares	Polytechnic Institute of Castelo Branco, Portugal
Thomas Strang	DLR, Germany
Markus Strassberger	BMW Group Research and Technology Germany
Jouni Tervonen	University of Oulu, Finland
Ozan Tonguz	Carnegie Mellon University, USA
Teresa Vazão	Inesc-ID/Instituto Superior Técnico, Portugal
Michelle Wetterwald	EURECOM, France

Technical Sponsors

- IFSTTAR, France
- Halmstad University, Sweden

Financial Sponsor

- Alcatel - Lucent Stiftung für Kommunikationsforschung

Table of Contents

Automotive Issues

Evaluation of WiFi for Kart Racing Monitoring.................... 1
   Harri Viittala, Matti Hämäläinen, Jari Iinatti, and Simone Soderi

Automated RF Emulator for a Highly Scalable IEEE802.11p
Communication and Localization Subsystem........................ 11
   Axel Sikora, Manuel Schappacher, and Lars Möllendorf

IEEE 802.15.4 Based Wireless Sensor Network for Automotive Test
and Measurement Applications with Predictable Frequency Agility..... 23
   Michael Binhack and Gerald Kupris

Car-to-Car

Context-Aware Retransmission Scheme for Increased Reliability
in Platooning Applications 30
   Annette Böhm, Magnus Jonsson, Kristina Kunert, and Alexey Vinel

An Improved Relevance Estimation Function for Cooperative
Awareness Messages in VANETs 43
   Jakob Breu and Michael Menth

Evaluation of Performance Enhancement for Crash Constellation
Prediction via Car-to-Car Communication: A Simulation Model Based
Approach 57
   Thomas Kuehbeck, Gor Hakobyan, Axel Sikora,
   Claude C. Chibelushi, and Mansour Moniri

Aviation Issues

Performance Evaluation of an Ethernet-Based Cabin Network
Architecture Supporting a Low-Latency Service 69
   Fabien Geyer, Stefan Schneele, and Wolfgang Fischer

Aeronautical Ad Hoc Network for Civil Aviation 81
   Quentin Vey, Alain Pirovano, José Radzik, and Fabien Garcia

A DDS-Based Middleware for Cooperation of Air Traffic Service
Units 94
   Erwin Mayer and Johannes Fröhlich

In-Car

Reliability Analysis of ZigBee Based Intra-Vehicle Wireless Sensor
Networks 103
    Md. Arafatur Rahman

Attack Potential and Efficient Security Enhancement of Automotive
Bus Networks Using Short MACs with Rapid Key Change 113
    Sebastian Bittl

Infrastructures

Optimization for Wireless Vehicular Network System in Urban Area.... 126
    Tsutomu Tsuboi and Tatsuya Sekiguchi

LTE Micro-cell Deployment for High-Density Railway Areas 143
    Aleksander Sniady, Mohamed Kassab, José Soler, and
    Marion Berbineau

Live Video Streaming in Vehicular Networks 156
    Alexey Vinel, Evgeny Belyaev, Boris Bellalta, and Honglin Hu

Author Index 163

Evaluation of WiFi for Kart Racing Monitoring

Harri Viittala[1], Matti Hämäläinen[1], Jari Iinatti[1], and Simone Soderi[2]

[1] Centre for Wireless Communications, University of Oulu, Oulu, Finland
{harri.viittala,matti.hamalainen,jari.iinatti}@oulu.fi
[2] GE Transportation Systems, Florence, Italy
simone.soderi@ge.com

Abstract. The focus of this paper is to study the throughput and jitter performances of the IEEE 802.11-2012 standard based solution for monitoring young kart racing drivers. At the low-level of kart racing, the speed of a kart is about 80 km/h. The PropSim channel emulator is applied to study performance of standard compliant radios in a vehicular environment. We will also study the impact of interference and shadowing on the system performance. The results indicate that it is feasible to use low-cost radios based on the IEEE 802.11 standards for this specific application if the need for bandwidth is not in Mbps.

Keywords: Communication, Karting, WiFi.

1   Introduction

Kart racing is a form of motorsport where vehicles are open and four-wheeled, namely karts. It is the most popular motorsport among youngsters and used commonly as the stepping stone to higher and more expensive classes of motorsport. The Finnish Formula One champions, Keke Rosberg, Mika Häkkinen and Kimi Räikkönen, all started their careers in kart racing. There are several classes covering different age groups in karting. It is typically started at the age of 6-7 years; and, after the age of 10, the first national competitions are available. At this level, the karts are reaching top speeds of about 80 km/h. The top-level of karting is KF1 which is open to the best drivers aged 15 and up. It is possible to reach top speeds up to 140 km/h and 70 km/h, on average, with this level of karts depending on the racing circuit layout. [1]

The length of homologated circuits varies between 748 m and 1700 m and is typically compacted into a small area. For example, the karting circuit located in Pori, Finland has a circuit length of 1045 m and outer dimensions of about 250 m x 200 m. [2]

At the lowest level of karting, driving skills are the most valuable asset because the karts are very similar to each other in terms of performance. By analyzing driver's actions when entering and exiting a curve, development of a young driver can be enhanced. Since the first classes of karting are the most low-budgeted, a need for an affordable, easy-to-deploy, reliable and portable monitoring system is present.

WiFi based on the 802.11 standards is a mature technology providing reliable communication and broad coverage with reasonably priced commercial components,

A. Sikora et al. (Eds.): Nets4Cars/Nets4Trains/Nets4Aircraft 2014, LNCS 8435, pp. 1–10, 2014.

and availability of the components makes fast adaptation possible. The schema of the monitoring system is depicted in Fig. 1. A karting circuit is typically an open-space without any major blocking objects. By using WiFi, one access point (AP) can basically cover a whole kart racing circuit. If connection is lost, the driving information is stored locally and transmitted right after a connection recovery. An analysis of the driver's performance is performed in a service area or pit.

The 802.11 physical (PHY) layer, i.e., orthogonal frequency division multiplexing (OFDM) defined in [3] has shown its strength as a PHY layer for vehicle-to-vehicle (V2V) and vehicle-to-infrastructure (V2I) communications. The 802.11a amendment was used as a basis for the 802.11p amendment which is applied as a PHY layer of wireless access in vehicular environment (WAVE) applications [4]. WAVE uses the 5.9 GHz frequency band dedicated for road safety, and includes V2V and V2I communications [4]. The 802.11p amendment uses licensed 5.9 GHz frequency band [4].

Due to price and use of licensed frequency band of the 802.11p, it is not feasible to low-cost driving analysis application. The present study focuses on the performance of commercial, affordable, off-the-shelf (COTS) WiFi radios in a vehicular environment. The paper is organized as follows: Section 2 presents the related work, Section 3 introduces the measurement setup, and Section 3 continues with the discussion on measurement parameters. In Section 4, the results from the measurement campaign are presented and analyzed. Finally, the paper is concluded in Section 5.

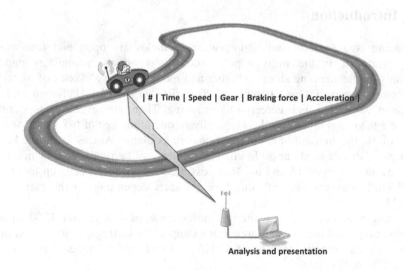

| # | Time | Speed | Gear | Braking force | Acceleration |

Analysis and presentation

Fig. 1. Schema of the kart monitoring system

2   Related Work

In [5], it is studied the throughput efficiency and the average delay performance of the IEEE 802.11 by using a Markov chain model. The OPNET simulations were carried out with the packet size of 1500 bytes having the channel bit rate of 11 Mbps. The results show that the throughput efficiency is 57.7 % for two stations with the contention window (CW) size of 32. Doubling the CW size decreases the throughput efficiency 3.5 percentage points. When the number stations are increased from 2 to 6, it has a slight influence on the throughput efficiency.

An analytical model for the enhanced distribution channel access (EDCA) mechanism in the IEEE 802.11p MAC layer is proposed in [6]. The model is validated against simulations. The model takes into account different features of EDCA, such as CW, different access classes (AC) and internal collisions. The normalized throughput was approximately 45% in the simulations where the packet payload was 512 bytes and the channel rate was 6 Mbps The measurements where the suitability of the IEEE 802.11 standard for the V2I communication is evaluated are presented in [7]. The user datagram protocol (UDP) throughput was measured with 802.11g and 802.11b also comparing different packet sizes. A fixed access point (AP) was passed with a car speeding up to 120 km/h. The authors concluded that the throughput is slightly smaller with this speed than in a static case showing that IEEE 802.11 is feasible for such velocities.

The WAVE performance measurement results for a V2I link are given in [8], where frame success ratio (FSR) is measured with various modulation-coding schemes, packet lengths and velocities. The maximum coverage of 700 m was reported for FSR > 0.25 at the data rate of 3 Mbps.

The V2I measurement results where the IEEE 802.11a and 802.11p are compared are reported in [9]. The packet size was set to 100 bytes. The connection time between a roadside unit (RSU) and a car was much longer when 802.11p was used, mainly because 802.11p does not require any authentication process, whereas it is needed to 802.11a to establish connection. In addition, it was found out that the packet losses of 802.11p were lower than 802.11a. The measurement devices applied the nominal channel bandwidths which are 10 MHz and 20 MHz for 802.11p and 802.11a, respectively. The selection of smaller bandwidth doubles the timing parameters of 802.11 improving the system performance in channels with a high delay spread. It is also possible to use 10 MHz bandwidth with 802.11a [3].

In our study, the focus is to evaluate if the affordable COTS WiFi radios are capable to perform in a vehicular environment.

3   Measurement Setup

The measurement setup contains commercial off-the-shelf (COTS) WiFi radios, a PropSim channel emulator [10], and laptops as illustrated in Fig. 2. One of the WiFi radios is tuned to work as an AP and another as a station (STA). Antenna connectors of the radios are connected to the PropSim so that 2x2 multiple-input multiple-output (MIMO) channels for an uplink and a downlink are formed. The throughput and jitter performance are measured by using the Iperf network testing tool installed in each laptop which, in turn, are connected to each radio with Ethernet cables. The WiFi radios are compliant with the IEEE802.11-2012 standard without optional features such as space-time block coding (STBC).

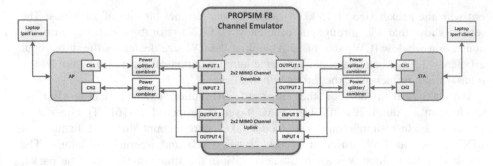

Fig. 2. Measurement setup

3.1   Ipert Network Testing Tool

The Iperf client generates 300 bytes user datagram protocol (UDP) data packets with a specified rate of 10 Mbps in this study. The packet size covers the data to be transmitted at the application layer. The Iperf server computes throughput, jitter and packet loss at an application layer. It counts lost datagrams based on an ID number of each datagrams. The size of the UDP packet varies between 8 – 65 535 bytes and usually consists of several internet protocol (IP) packets. Losing one IP packet will lose the whole UDP packet. The UDP packet size was set to 300 bytes. When the maximum transmission unit (MTU) is 1500 bytes, we can call a datagram as a packet, and the number of lost datagrams is equal to lost packets. [11]

3.2   PropSim Channel Emulator

A channel emulator is applied to model a wireless channel for studying performance of real hardware. Complex set-ups can be built in a laboratory environment so as to closely emulate a real scenario. The emulation is based on pre-calculated files, i.e., channel impulse response and other related parameters. The PropSim channel emulator includes several standard channel models; but, it is also possible to create a unique channel model when needed parameters are known. [10]

A work flow with PropSim starts by defining a channel impulse response tap by tap. For each channel tap, properties such as delay, amplitude distribution, Doppler spread, correlation, etc. can be adjusted. The next step is to connect a generated channel to RF inputs and outputs. Finally, the channel is emulated and measurements can be done.

V2I Channel Model

Our V2I channel model is based on the roadside-to-vehicle (RTV) Expressway channel model at 5.9 GHz presented in [12]. All parameters needed for channel emulation are presented in Table 1.

Table 1. Channel model for RTV-Expressway

Tap no.	Path no.	Tap power [dB]	Relative path loss [dB]	Delay value [ns]	Rician K [dB]	Frequency shift [Hz]	Fading Doppler [Hz]	LOS Doppler [Hz]	Fading spectral shape
1	1	0.0	0.0	0	-5.3	769	70	770	Round
1	2	0.0	-36.4	1	n/a	-22	600	n/a	Round
1	3	0.0	-30.0	2	n/a	535	376	n/a	Round
2	4	-9.3	-12.3	100	n/a	754	117	n/a	Round
2	5	-9.3	-21.7	101	n/a	548	424	n/a	Round
2	6	-9.3	-24.9	102	n/a	-134	530	n/a	Flat
3	7	-20.3	-24.3	200	n/a	761	104	n/a	Round
3	8	-20.3	-25.4	201	n/a	88	813	n/a	Classic 3 dB
4	9	-21.3	-26.8	300	n/a	37	802	n/a	Classic 6 dB
4	10	-21.3	-28.5	301	n/a	752	91	n/a	Round
5	11	-28.8	-31.2	400	n/a	16	807	n/a	Classic 6 dB
5	12	-28.8	-41.8	401	n/a	-755	329	n/a	Round

Interference

In PropSim, there is also functionality to internally generate an interfering signal. A preliminary interference test was done by adding the filtered additive white Gaussian noise (AWGN) with constant signal-to-noise power ratio (SNR) for each received antenna.

Shadowing

It is also possible to add slow fading to the channel emulating the effect of obstacles in the signal path. A shadowing feature of PropSim was applied to test the system response when an attenuation of a channel is increased. The channel gain was decreased with 0.1 s time intervals to -35 dB or -50 dB. After a breakpoint, the gain was increased back to 0 dB.

4   Measurement Parameters

During measurements, the radios were adjusted to use the 802.11a+n radio protocol with 5745 MHz channel center frequency and 5 dBm transmitted power which was the minimum available power level. Single-input single-output (SISO) and MIMO setups were applied. The radios did not have a support for STBC or other diversity methods. The transport protocol was UDP with a packet size of 300 bytes and a bandwidth of 10 Mbps. During a 3-minute measurement run, about 750 000 UDP packets were transmitted. In an interference measurement, a possible interference source is co-located exactly in the channel of a victim system covering the victim frequency band completely or partially. Two values of the maximum shadowing attenuation were applied, namely 35 dB and 50 dB. All the parameters are summarized in Table 2.

Table 2. Measurement parameters

Parameter	Value
Radio protocol	802.11a+n
Frequency channel	5.745 GHz (#149)
Channel bandwidth	20 MHz
Transmitted power	5 dBm
Transport protocol	UDP
UDP packet size	300 B
UDP bandwidth	10 Mbps
Velocity	10, 50, 100 or 140 km/h
Interference center frequency	5.745 GHz
Interference bandwidth	5 or 20 MHz
SNR in interference measurement	10 or 15 dB
Maximum attenuation in shadowing measurement	35 or 50 dB

The link quality given by the software driver of the WiFi board was recorded before emulation to confirm operation of the setup. As it can be seen from Table 3, connections were perfectly functional in SISO and MIMO setups.

Table 3. Link quality before channel emulation

Setup	SISO	MIMO
Link quality	70/70	70/70
Bit rate	65 Mbps (MCS7)	130 Mbps (MCS15)
Signal level	-34 dBm	-35 dBm

5   Results

The results of the measurements are discussed in this chapter. The throughput and jitter performances of the system were measured at the application layer. The impact of velocity, interference and shadowing were studied to have a comprehensive understanding of the system performance.

5.1   Velocity

The performances of SISO and MIMO setups were measured by using velocities of 10, 50, 100 and 140 km/h. The corresponding maximum Doppler shifts are 53, 266, 531 and 745 Hz. The measurement results are presented in Fig. 3 and Fig. 4. A line represents an average result, whereas a bar depicts a standard deviation. For both setups, it is clear that when the velocity increases from 10 km/h to 50 km/h, the throughput performance degrades dramatically. In the end, the MIMO setup gives the mean throughput of 1199 kbps with 140 km/h, and correspondingly 491 kbps for SISO. The jitter performance is in reasonable range in the case of MIMO for all studied velocities, whereas it varies strongly for SISO. The IEEE 802.11-2012 standard defines the subcarrier spacing of the 20 MHz OFDM PHY to be 312.5 kHz [3]. With velocity of 50 km/h, the intercarrier interference (ICI) starts to have an impact on the system performance. An extensive study on the effect of Doppler spread on the OFDM system performance can be found, e.g., in [13].

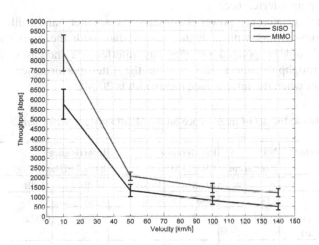

Fig. 3. Impact of velocity on the system throughput performance

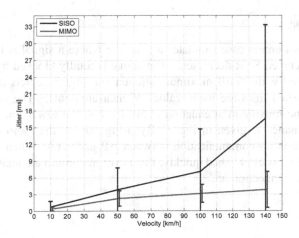

Fig. 4. Impact of velocity on the system jitter performance

5.2   Interference

In public spaces such as a karting circuit, there may also exist other WiFi devices or other equipment using the same frequency band. These introduce interference to the desired system. The performance of the system was measured by using two possible interfering systems having the channel bandwidth of 20 MHz and 5 MHz. The interference was modeled as a band-limited white Gaussian noise. Table 4 gives the mean results and standard deviation values (σ) of the measurements for different the signal-to-interference power ratios (SIR). The results show that the system manages interference overlapping communication bandwidth completely better than partially overlapping interference.

When the total interference power is constant, the smaller bandwidth interference interferes less sub-carriers with at higher power than with the higher interference bandwidth. It should be pointed out that any interference increases the standard deviation in throughput almost 100 %. In the jitter performance, there is no significant impact when the interference bandwidth is 20 MHz.

Table 4. Impact of interference on the MIMO system performance

Parameter	No interference	Interference BW=20 MHz		Interference BW=5 MHz	
SIR	∞	10 dB	15 dB	10 dB	15 dB
Mean throughput [kbps] (σ)	8337 (868)	6934 (1742)	8701 (1519)	3256 (1574)	5559 (1372)
Mean jitter [ms] (σ)	0.42 (0.39)	0.44 (0.26)	0.40 (0.54)	2.75 (8.50)	0.91 (2.85)

5.3   Shadowing

This MIMO measurement case simulates a situation where a signal is blocked by an obstacle and a received SNR decreases. The signal is totally blocked by using 50 dB or partially blocked with 35 dB maximum attenuation. Fig. 5 depicts the throughput results, where dashed lines are mean values of measurements. The upper figure is the case where the maximum attenuation is 50 dB, and the lower one is for 35 dB. The jitter performance is given in Fig. 6. By using 50 dB, the radio link is totally blocked and there is no communication between AP and STA. When attenuation is low enough, the link is established quickly. For lower maximum attenuation, the radio is able to keep the connection up.

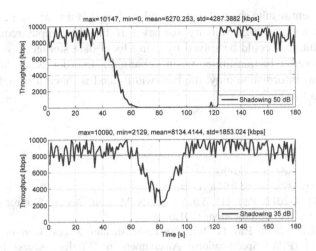

Fig. 5. Impact of shadowing on the system throughput performance

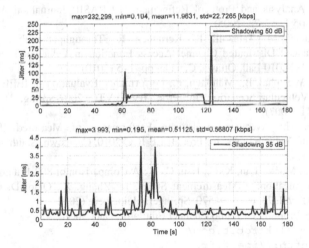

Fig. 6. Impact of shadowing on the system jitter performance

6   Conclusion

This paper presented the measurement results where radio system performance was studied in the vehicular environment. The karting monitoring system is needed to provide a possibility to monitor and analyze performance of young drivers in the early stages of their professional careers. The lower level of kart racing has the lowest budget, and hence costs should be minimal. The radio system based on WiFi allows the opportunity for monitoring and analysis by providing affordably priced hardware options.

The measurement results showed that a standard-based WiFi, without any optional features, cannot manage high velocity scenarios if the throughput requirement is several Mbps. But, this could be solved by using local data storage in a kart where information is stored to be transmitted when a channel is in order. Nevertheless, when transmitting status information only, the bandwidth need is much less and the radios can operate up to 140 km/h.

References

1. AKK, http://www.autourheilu.fi/
2. CIK-FIA, http://www.cikfia.com/
3. IEEE Std 802.11-2012: Part 11: Wireless LAN Medium Access Control (MAC) and Physical Layer (PHY) Specifications (2012)
4. IEEE Std 802.11p-2010: Part 11: Wireless LAN Medium Access Control (MAC) and Physical Layer (PHY) Specifications: Amendment 6: Wireless Access in Vehicular Environments (2010)
5. Chatzimisios, P., Boucouvalas, A.C., Vitsas, V.: IEEE 802.11 Wireless LANs: Performance Analysis and Protocol Refinement. EURASIP Journal on Applied Signal Processing 2005 1, 67–78 (2005)
6. Han, C., Dianati, M., Tafazolli, R., Kernchen, R.: Throughput analysis of the IEEE 802.11p Enhanced Distributed Channel Access Function in Vehicular Environment. In: Proc. IEEE VTC 2010-Fall, Ottawa, Canada, pp. 1–5 (2010)
7. Wellens, M., Westphal, B., Mähönen, P.: Performance Evaluation of IEEE 802.11-based WLANs in Vehicular Scenarios. In: Proc. IEEE VTC 2007-Spring, Dublin, Ireland, pp. 1167–1171 (2007)
8. Paier, A., et al.: Average Downstream Performance of Measured IEEE 802.11p Infrastructure-to-Vehicle Links. In: Proc. IEEE ICC 2010, Capetown, South Africa, pp. 1–5 (2010)
9. Lin, W.-Y., Li, M.-W., Lan, K.-C., Hsu, C.-H.: A Comparison of 802.11a and 802.11p for V-to-I Communication: A Measurement Study. In: Zhang, X., Qiao, D. (eds.) QShine 2010. LNICST, vol. 74, pp. 559–570. Springer, Heidelberg (2012)
10. Elektrobit, EB PropSim F8 Radio Channel Emulator, Data Sheet, http://www.elektrobit.com/
11. Iperf Forum, http://iperf.fr/
12. Acosta-Marum, G., Ingram, M.A.: Six Time- and Frequency-Selective Empirical Channel Models for Vehicular Wireless LANs. IEEE Vehicular Technology Magazine 2(4), 4–11 (2007)
13. Wang, T., Proakis, J.G., Masry, E., Zeidler, J.R.: Performance Degradation of OFDM Systems Due to Doppler Spreading. IEEE Trans. Wireless Comm. 5(6), 1422–1432 (2006)

Automated RF Emulator for a Highly Scalable IEEE802.11p Communication and Localization Subsystem

Axel Sikora[1], Manuel Schappacher[2], and Lars Möllendorf[2]

[1] Offenburg University of Applied Sciences,
Faculty of Electrical & Information Technology Engineering, Offenburg, Germany
axel.sikora@hs-offenburg.de

[2] Steinbeis Innovation Center Embedded Design and Networking, Heitersheim, Germany
{manuel.schappacher,lars.moellendorf}@stzedn.de

Abstract. The IEEE802.11p standard describes a protocol for car-to-X and mainly for car-to-car-communication. In the research project Ko-TAG, which is part of the research initiative Ko-FAS, cooperative sensor technology is developed for the support of highly autonomous driving. The Ko-TAG subsystem improves the real-time characteristics of IEEE802.11p needed for precise time of flight real-time localization while still fitting into the regulatory schemes. A secondary radar principle based on communication signals enables localization of objects with simultaneous data transmission. The Ko-TAG subsystem mainly concentrates on the support of traffic safety applications in intra-urban scenarios. This paper details on the development of a fully automated RF emulator used to test the Ko-TAG subsystem.

The RF emulator includes the physical networking nodes, but models the RF environment using RF-waveguides. The RF emulator allows the controlling of path loss and connectivity between any of the nodes with the help of RF attenuators and programmable RF switches, while it is shielded against its surrounding RF environment in the lab. Therefore it is an inexpensive alternative to an RF absorber chamber, which often is not available or exceeds the project's budget.

Details about the system definition can be found in earlier papers. Test results are shown in the last part of the paper.

Keywords: Car-2-Car communication, Car-2-X communication, emulation, IEEE802.11p/WAVE, subsystem design, VRU eSafety, localization, real time, secondary surveillance radar, standardization.

1 Introduction

The IEEE802.11p standard has developed as the most popular basis for Car-to-X-(C2X)-communication [1]. For the USA, the "IEEE 1609 Family of Standards for Wireless Access in Vehicular Environment (WAVE)" [2] defines an architecture and a complementary, standardized set of services and interfaces that collectively enable

A. Sikora et al. (Eds.): Nets4Cars/Nets4Trains/Nets4Aircraft 2014, LNCS 8435, pp. 11–22, 2014.

secure Car-to-Car (C2C) and Car-to-Infrastructure (C2I) wireless communications. IEEE802.11p is also to be used as the platform for Dedicated Short Range Communications (DSRC), a U.S. Department of Transportation (DoT) project based on the ISO Communications, Air-interface, Long and Medium range (CALM) architecture standard. It is targeted at vehicle-based communication networks, particularly for applications such as toll collection, vehicle safety services, and commerce transactions via cars.

The European activities are also based on IEEE802.11p Wireless LAN. A frequency spectrum in the 5.9 GHz range has been allocated on a harmonized basis in Europe [3] in line with similar allocations in USA. Here the higher layers are defined by the Car2Car Communication Consortium [4]. Car2X communication technology enables a number of new use cases in order to improve driving safety or traffic efficiency and provides information or entertainment to the driver [2]. IEEE802.11p has found its place in hardware and firmware implementations, and is currently extensively tested in various large-scale field tests, i.e. in the German simTD test field [5].

This work results from the joint project Ko-TAG, which is part of the project initiative Ko-FAS [6], and has been partially funded by the German Bundesministerium für Wirtschaft und Technologie (Federal Department of Commerce and Technology) under contract number 19S9011.

The remainder of this paper is organized as follows:

Section 2 will shortly discuss how the Ko-TAG project overcomes the limitations in scalability and real-time location capability of the IEEE802.11p/WAVE-protocol.

Section 3 describes an automated RF emulator that uses physical networking nodes, but still models the RF environment using RF-waveguides.

Section 4 presents results from measurements in the emulator.

This paper is an extension to [9], where the design flow and the testbed from the same project are described in more detail and to [13] that details on the Ko-TAG subsystem. This paper concentrates on the development of an automated emulator of the Ko-TAG subsystem and the quantitative results of the emulation.

2   Ko-TAG Subsystem Improving the Real-Time Characteristics of IEEE802.11p

The IEEE802.11p amendment has developed as the most popular basis for C2X-communication [1]. It can be understood as a refinement of the IEEE802.11a/h standards targeted at vehicle-based communications to support Intelligent Transportation Systems (ITS) applications. IEEE802.11p allows data exchange between high-speed vehicles and between the vehicles and the roadside infrastructure but it is not fitted for collision avoidance systems. As the Ko-TAG subsystem is focused on traffic safety applications in intra-urban scenarios including pre-crash safety, the characteristics of the target application are very different from the capabilities of both IEEE802.11a and p. I.e. three requirements are critical: (1) real-time characteristics, (2) density and scalability and (3) support and accuracy of localization.

The Ko-TAG subsystem extends the current IEEE802.11p protocols and follows the communication model of secondary surveillance radar from air traffic control. Thus, it combines communication and localization and has been designed to work as an add-on subsystem, which may be seamlessly integrated both into IEEE802.11p-based car-to-X-communication or into sensor fusion together with image-based systems, like e.g.

[7] [8]. The technology can also be used for an omnidirectional perception system for pre-crash safety and as sensor support for intersection safety.

Within the Ko-TAG-architecture, vehicles are equipped with a Localization Unit (LU), which communicates with RF transponders called SafeTAGs (ST). Such a ST can be given to any secondary partner, e.g. Vulnerable Raod Users (VRU), other vehicles or parts of the infrastructure like traffic lights at intersections [12]. The sensor concept allows for a selective localization of STs and a selective communication link between LUs and STs for an efficient use of the available bandwidth. Furthermore there is a lightly modified version of the ST that can be connected to an LU via a TCP/IP link to provide omnidirectional safety amongst vehicles. The hardware design includes the complete system design from RF-frontend over signal processing, network operation until Gigabit-Ethernet-interfacing to the vehicle's Fusion Unit (FU).

The communication is organized in super frames, in which communication and localization between various pairs are organized. The channel access divides into three phases, which can be multiplexed in various dimensions, i.e. time and frequency:

1. a detection and network management phase, when VRU tags can register to vehicles.
2. a time of flight (TOF) measurement phase, which is extremely time critical, as clock drifts between measurement partners lead to localization errors.
3. an angle of arrival (AOA) measurement phase, which can be used in parallel for data communication.

Thus, the channel access combines contention periods for arbitrary and management traffic, and contention free periods (reserved time slots) for time- and collision-critical operations. The physical breakup into the different frequencies helps to solve the conflict of objectives with regard to bandwidth requirements.

3   The Ko-TAG Emulator

3.1   Emulation Benefits

As soon as the hardware prototypes are available, there is the need to reproducibly test the hardware and the protocol. In practice, in a project like Ko-TAG, hardware and protocol are developed in parallel. This is particularly true, if an iterative spiral development model is used [9].

Simulation is used to test the behavior of the protocol and its implementation, i.e. the firmware on hardware abstraction layer level. The advantage of simulation is its scalability. In the Ko-TAG project simulation has been used to prove that the proposed system is well scalable and can deal with more than 200 VRUs in the neighborhood of one vehicle ("cell size") [13]. However, as the hardware is not part of the simulation it is not suitable for the iterative development model used in the project to co-develop the hard- and firmware.

1. Simulation is not helpful in debugging the underlying hardware.
2. Simulation is totally missing the effects that hardware has on RF characteristics.

Outdoor field-tests are indispensable for testing the capabilities and reliability of the overall system, but they are not suitable for the iterative development model as well:

1. Outdoor field tests are not reproducible because of the uncontrollable nature of the outdoor environment, i.e. reflectors for multi-path propagation.
2. Outdoor field tests are time consuming and therefore expensive.

This paper describes the development of a testing environment that includes the hardware and allows controlling the environment. The alternative, an RF absorber chamber, often is not available or exceeds the project's budget. So the idea is to develop an emulator, where physical networking nodes are used, but where the RF environment is still modeled using RF-waveguides. In such an environment, it is well possible e.g. to control the path loss between any of the nodes with the help of RF attenuators and to control the connectivity between any of the nodes with the help of programmable RF switches. This emulator can be used at a first stage to check the system's behavior under given circumstances. At the second stage the corresponding test can be reproduced to verify the impact e.g. of changes in the firmware made to improve the performance.

3.2   Emulator Hardware

Fig. 1 shows the logical setup of the Ko-TAG emulator platform, where the Ko-TAG RF nodes are mounted into shielded boxes (cf. Fig. 4) and are interconnected via RF-waveguides, splitters, and attenuation elements. The signals at the LU can be observed via a Signal Analyzer (Agilent EXA N9010A). Additional noise and signals can be fed into the RF channel from the Vector Signal Generator (Agilent MXG N5182A). The Vector Signal Generator can work continuously, but can also be triggered, so that the interference can be inserted in relation to the overall time synchronization.

The local control of the RF switches and thus the control of the RF paths is performed by an ARM Cortex-M3 based microcontroller unit (STM32F107VCT6). Based on the experience from earlier emulator setups, all elements are carefully mounted and additionally shielded. The links are fixed with a torque wrench. All elements and connections are characterized after they have been built-in with regard to attenuation, reflection, and phase shift (delay).

3.3   Emulator Software

All involved devices, the Measurement Devices (MD), the RF-Switch Controller (RfSC) and the Ko-TAG RF nodes i.e. Devices Under Test (DUT) are controlled and monitored by a MATLAB program from a PC. The MD can be programmed using Standard Commands for Programmable Instruments (SCPI) over LAN eXtensions for Instrumentation (LXI). As MATLAB provides the usage of external programming interfaces, Java IO libraries (java.io.PrintWriter / java.io.BufferedReader) are used to send the SCPI commands to the devices directly out of MATLAB. The RfSC is fitted with the STZEDN's embedded TCP/IP protocol suite (emBetter) which is expanded by an SCPI module. Therefore the aforementioned MATLAB SCPI interface can be used to control the RF switches as well. The same emBetter based implementation provides the DUT with SCPI capability.

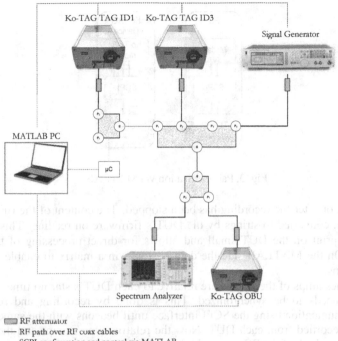

Ko-TAG TAG ID1   Ko-TAG TAG ID3

Signal Generator

MATLAB PC

μC

Spectrum Analyzer   Ko-TAG OBU

▭ RF attenuator
— RF path over RF coax cables
···· SCPI configuration and control via MATLAB
    RF switch controlled by μC

Fig. 1. Logical topology of Ko-TAG emulator

Fig. 2. Physical topology of Ko-TAG emulator

Additionally the firmware of the DUT is extended by a ring buffer to store information about every frame send or received to enable asynchronous delivery of the recorded packages. In general the timestamp of sending or reception of the frame is saved along with its cycle and slot within the Ko-TAG super frame, its frame type and a frame type specific content. The SCPI commands allow start and stop of the recording. It also supports the continuous reading of the content from the ring buffer in parallel to

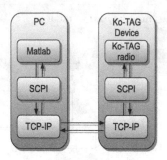

Fig. 3. Parametrisation via MATLAB

the recording or after the recording has been stopped. The content of the ring buffer is serialized, i.e. converted to strings by the DUT's firmware on reading. This keeps the memory footprint on the DUT small and allows for direct processing of the data in MATLAB. On the MATLAB side the data is stored in a matrix to enable vectorized data operations.

As the timestamps of the frames are relative to each DUT's startup time, the timing information needs to be synchronized. This is done by recording and reading the DUT's communication using the SCPI interface until beacons with the same sequence number are recorded from each DUT. Now the relative time stamps and their off sets to the real time clock of the PC are used to calculate the absolute time.

An automated test run is fully defined by a MATLAB script that starts the synchronization, configures the MDs and the signal generator, controls the status of the RF-switches, starts the recording phases for each test sample, collects the data from all DUTs, and generates diagrams based on the collected data. Once the emulator hardware is set up, i.e. all devices are mounted the automated test can be repeated with one call to this script.

4   Results

4.1   Specification of the Test Cases

The tests are executed automatically as described in chapter 3. The DUT are mounted to emulators RF waveguides. Before the test runs a reference measurement is taken. All open RF waveguides are closed by 50 Ohm terminators. To get an impression of the possibilities provided by the emulator here is a summary of the test cases defined for the Ko-TAG project:

1. To test the communication under different path attenuations, a RF node pair consisting of one LU and one ST is mounted to the emulator's waveguides. The emulator then switches between 8 paths with different attenuations ranging from 48 dB to 110 dB. The packet success rate is calculated to show that the system is stable at the specific attenuation condition.

2. To test the communication under shadowing effects the emulator switches paths from low attenuation (e.g. 48 dB) to high attenuation (82 dB) for 10 seconds and

then back to low attenuation. The packet success rate is calculated to show that the system is stable under abrupt shadowing effects. This test is repeated for various attenuation levels (64/72 dB, 48/82 dB, 69/110 dB).

3. To test the time of flight (TOF) and angle of arrival/data (AOA/Data) communication the corresponding channels are interfered by continuous additive white Gaussian noise (AWGN) under different path attenuation. The emulator triggers the signal generator to activate an AWGN signal on the communication path with increasing power level. The packet success rate is calculated to show that the system is stable up to a specific noise level. This test is repeated for various attenuation levels (84 dB, 74 dB, 64 dB, 54 dB) and those test runs are done twice, one for each channel (TOF, AOA/Data).

4. To test the TOF communication under interference by a narrow band signal under different path attenuation (64 dB, 84 dB) the same setup as in test case 3 is used but here the signal generator emits a modulated narrow band signal.

5. To show that the system also stays stable for more than one ST, the setup of test case 3 is repeated with two STs.

6. To test the TOF and AOA/Data communication between one LU and two STs under interference by a modulated wide band signal the setup of test case 5 is reused. Here the signal generator emits a signal which characteristics resemble those of WIMAX radio.

7. To test the communication under intrinsic interference two STs and one LU are mounted to the emulator's waveguides like in the test cases 5 and 6. This time there is no interference by the signal generator, but both STs are sending in the same time slot under varying path attenuation conditions.

Because of the limited space, this publication only shows the results of two of the test cases in chapter 4.2.

4.2   Analyses of Test Results

Fig. 4 shows one sample result out of a series of 10 samples executed with the emulator during the automated run for the TOF channel of test case 5. The number of frames is assigned to the vertical axes. On the horizontal axes the bars are grouped for each of the two ST (TAG ID 1, TAG ID 3) and for both STs in total (ALL). Each group consist of a pair of bars for time of flight (TOF) frames (pink), Data frames (blue) and angle of arrival (AOA) frames (green). The filled bars depict the frames actually received. The bordered grey bars behind the filled ones depict the corresponding number of expected frames. The numbers are also printed on the bars in the format: "received/expected (packet success rate)".

The intention of the test is to examine the behavior of three DUT, i.e. one LU and two STs under continuous AWGN with a bandwidth (BW) of 24 MHz and a center frequency (CF) of 5800 MHz which is the center of the TOF channel. The test case consists of 10 samples ([a] to [j]). The AWGN signal starts with a distance of 13 dB to the wanted signal in the first sample (sample [a]). Then the AWGN signal power increases in 2 dB steps until its distance to the wanted signal is -5 dB (sample [j]).

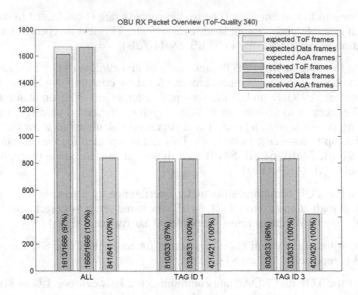

Fig. 4. Packet success rate for 2 DUTs (AWGN 24 MHz BW, 13 dB below wanted signal)

The summary of the 10 test samples in Fig. 5 shows how the packet success rate decreases with increasing power of the AWGN. The packet success rates are assigned to the vertical axis. On the horizontal axis each letter stands for a single test sample. The TOF channel of the Ko-TAG system stays stable until the distance of the AWGN to the wanted signal is below 11 dB. The other channels are not affected.

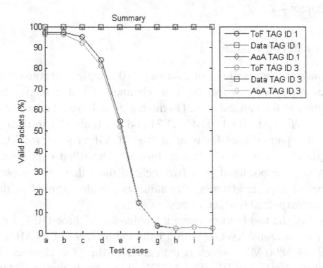

Fig. 5. Summary of test run with 1 LU and 2 ST disturbed by WGN   (CF 5800 MHz, BW 24 MHz, 13 to -5 dB distance to wanted signal)

The results of test scenario 7 are summarized in Fig. 6 to Fig. 9. In this scenario the behavior of the DUT under intrinsic interference is tested. Only the TOF channel is observed. Two ST (ID1 and ID3) are connected to one LU. ST ID1 should send in slot 1, ST ID3 should send in slot 3, but here both ST are sending in the same super frame slot 3. For the LU the two STs appear like one ST as it distinguishes them on the basis of their super frame slot. However, as the STs have different emulated spatial distances to the LU, in the diagrams the STs can be distinguished by the measured distance.

The diagrams are showing the TOF beacons (green circles) of the two ST received by the LU plotted into a three dimensional coordinate system. The quality indicator on the vertical axis refers to the quality of the RF signal received by the LU. In this case the TOF beacons with a quality below 340 are regarded as invalid. The distance values on the horizontal axis are not calibrated, but in this case the relative values are sufficient to distinguish the two ST. The third axis denotes the timestamps. The diagrams shown are rotated to give a clearer view on the transition of TOF packages received from ST ID1 to ST ID3.

An RF switch between the LU and each ST provides two different radio paths for each pair of devices. For ST ID1 one path (LOW) includes 13 dB, the other path (HIGH) includes 16 dB of additional attenuation. For ST ID3 one path (LOW) includes 13 dB, the other path (HIGH) includes 20 dB of additional attenuation.

Table 1. Intrinsic Interference test configurations

	CID			
Parameter	[a]	[b]	[c]	[d]
signal distance ST ID1 to 3	7 dB	4 dB	0 dB	-3 dB
RF-Path LU-ST ID1	LOW	HIGH	LOW	HIGH
RF-Path-LU-ST ID3	HIGH	HIGH	LOW	LOW

Table 1 shows the different test configurations, each configuration labeled with a configuration identifier (CID) [a] to [d]. The RF paths are switched for each CID to decrease the distance between the signal of ST ID1 and the signal of ST ID3.

Fig. 8 shows CID [a] in which the signal of ST ID3 is attenuated by 7 dB in comparison to the signal of ST ID1. Since both ST send in the same slot 3 the LU receives only noise in slot 1. The TOF beacons shown originate from ST ID1 as well as ST ID3. The not calibrated distance of ST ID3 to the LU is about 1554.5, the not calibrated distance of ST ID1 to the LU is about 1555.5. As the signal of ST ID1 is stronger than the signal of ST ID3 the valid TOF are scattered between the distances of both STs.

Fig. 7 shows CID [b] in which the signal of ST ID3 is only attenuated by 4 dB in comparison to the signal of ST ID1. It is interesting that the concentration of valid TOF beacons is moving towards the distance value of ST ID3, since its TOF are received better now.

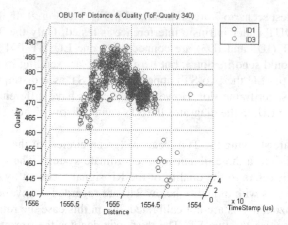

Fig. 6. Intrinsic interference test - CID [a]

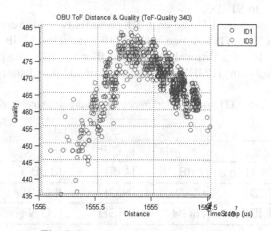

Fig. 7. Intrinsic interference test - CID [b]

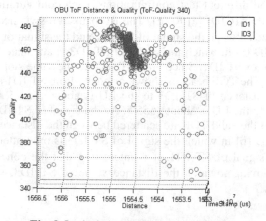

Fig. 8. Intrinsic interference test - CID [c]

Fig. 8 shows CID [c] in which case both ST signals have the same attenuation. The concentration of valid TOF beacons is closer to ST ID3, now.

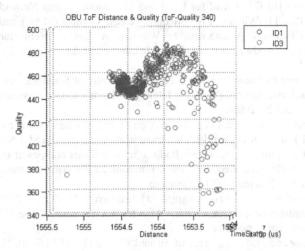

Fig. 9. Intrinsic interference test - CID [d]

Fig. 9 shows CID [d] in which case the signal of ST ID1 is attenuated by 3 dB in comparison to the signal of ST ID3. The distance values of the received TOF are now those of ST ID3.

This test shows that in case of intrinsic disturbance on the TOF channel, the signal of the interferer (ST ID1) has to be stronger than the wanted signal to invalidate the distance information.

5   Summary and Outlook

Within the Ko-TAG project, a subsystem to the IEEE802.11p Car-2-Car Communication was designed, implemented and tested, which allows the integration of real time communication and precise relative localization. Parts of the tests were conducted using a fully automated RF emulator. The measurement devices, the signal generator used as interferer, the status of the RF-switches that switch between different waveguides, the data collection from the devices under test and the generation of diagrams based on the collected data were all done using MATLAB to enable easy reproducibility of the tests.

The test results were very promising. They could be qualitatively verified in outdoor field tests, which were performed with typical conditions. A quantitative comparison is impossible, as in the field tests, the communication of the different devices cannot be synchronized as in the emulator.

References

1. 802.11p-2010 - IEEE Standard for Local and Metropolitan Area Networks - Specific requirements Part 11: Wireless LAN Medium Access Control (MAC) and Physical Layer (PHY) Specifications Amendment 6: Wireless Access in Vehicular Environments, http://standards.ieee.org/findstds/standard/802.11p-2010.html

2. U.S. Department of Transportation, IEEE 1609 - Family of Standards for Wireless Access in Vehicular Environments (WAVE), Intelligent Transportation Systems Standards Fact Sheet (September 25, 2009), http://www.standards.its.dot.gov/fact_sheet.asp?f=80

3. Harmonized European Standard (Telecommunication series), ETSI EN 302 571 V1.1.1: Intelligent Transport Systems (ITS); Radiocommunications equipment operating in the 5 855 MHz to 5 925 MHz frequency band; Harmonized EN covering the essential requirements of article 3.2 of the R&TTE Directive, http://pda.etsi.org/exchangefolder/en_302571v010101p.pdf

4. Car2Car Communication Consortium, "Manifesto Overview of the C2C-CC System", http://www.car-to-car.org

5. http://www.simtd.org/index.dhtml/114ecb33f716a062019p/-/enEN/-/CS/-/

6. http://www.kofas.de/

7. Andreone, L., Visintainer, F.: Prevention of road accidents involving Vulnerable Road Users: the outcomes of the WATCH-OVER European project. In: ITS 2009, Stockholm (2009)

8. Blume, H., Flügel, S., Kunert, M., Ritter, W., Sikora, A.: Mehr Sicherheit für Fußgänger: Überblick über das vom Bundesministerium für Bildung und Forschung (BMBF) geförderte Forschungsprojekt Propedes, Elektronik automotive 12 (2011)

9. Sikora, A., Lill, D., Schappacher, M., Gutjahr, S., Gerber, E.: Development of Car2X Communication and Localization PHY and MAC Protocol Following Iterative Spiral Model Using Simulation and Emulation

10. Mueller, M.: WLAN IEEE802.11p Measurements for Vehicle to Vehicle (V2V) DSRC, Application Note, Rohde & Schwarz 09.2009 1 MA152_Oe

11. Großmann, U., Schauch, M., Hakobyan, S.: The accuracy of algorithms for WLAN indoor positioning and the standardization of signal reception for different mobile devices. Int'l J. of Computing 6(I1), 103–109 (2007)

12. Lill, D., Schappacher, M., Islam, S., Sikora, A.: Wireless Protocol Design for a Cooperative Pedestrian Protection System. In: Strang, T., Festag, A., Vinel, A., Mehmood, R., Rico Garcia, C., Röckl, M. (eds.) Nets4Cars/Nets4Trains 2011. LNCS, vol. 6596, pp. 119–130. Springer, Heidelberg (2011)

13. Sikora, A., Schappacher, M.: A highly scalable IEEE802.11p communication and localization subsystem for autonomous urban driving. In: International Conference on Connected Vehicles and Expo 2013, ICCVE 2013 (2013)

14. Staub, T., Gantenbein, R., Braun, T.: VirtualMesh: an emulation framework for wireless mesh networks in OMNeT++. In: 2nd Int'l Conference on Simulation Tools and Techniques, Simutools 2009 (2009)

15. Evans, N.S., Grothoff, C.: Beyond simulation: large-scale distributed emulation of P2P protocols. In: 4th Conference on Cyber Security Experimentation and Test, CSET 2011 (2011)

16. Iwanicki, K., Gaba, A., van Steen, M.: KonTest: A Wireless Sensor Network Testbed at Vrije Universiteit Amsterdam, Technical Report IR-CS-045 (August 2008), http://www.few.vu.nl/~iwanicki/ (visited December 2012)

IEEE 802.15.4 Based Wireless Sensor Network
for Automotive Test and Measurement Applications
with Predictable Frequency Agility

Michael Binhack[1] and Gerald Kupris[2]

[1] senTec Elektronik GmbH, Werner-von-Siemens-Str. 6, 98693 Ilmenau, Germany
[2] Technische Hochschule Deggendorf, Edlmairstraße 6 und 8, 94469 Deggendorf, Germany
michael.binhack@sentec-elektronik.de,
gerald.kupris@th-deg.de

Abstract. IEEE 802.15.4 [1] is a standard on which many industrial, commercial and residential applications were based on. Devices designed for this standard are characterized for long battery lifetime, small data bandwidth and low cost.

Test and measurement equipment for automotive applications based on IEEE 802.15.4 have those advantages. Also disadvantages according coexistence towards other wireless technologies in fast moving equipment are discussed and solutions in a test application to measure temperatures on brake disks are presented. Especially for very dynamic measurements a strong increase of reliability can be realized with predictable frequency agility.

Keywords: IEEE 802.15.4, automotive, WSN, wireless test equipment.

1 Introduction

Short range WSN (wireless sensor networks) in cars means mainly Bluetooth for infotainment and often proprietary technologies for on board diagnostics as tire pressure monitoring or passive open and entry systems. One of the most popular short range technologies IEEE 802.15.4 and several standards based on it like ZigBee™ [2] or WirelessHART™ [3] are not used in automotive applications. One of the most important differences of a wireless system in a car towards stationary systems in industrial or residential applications is the fast changing influence of external interferences. Especially in the worldwide free 2.4 GHz band many other wireless technologies can be found. Nearly all investigations about coexistence of different wireless technologies were done in fixed and quasi static environmental conditions. Also the offered solutions to handle coexistence conflicts were mainly developed for fixed conditions.

With a fast moving system those coexistence solutions are not always suitable for best system performance. E.g. a frequency management with distribution of several frequencies for each participant in the used frequency band is worthless for a moving application. Here a flexible solution like predictable frequency agility is necessary to handle the fast changing interferences.

A. Sikora et al. (Eds.): Nets4Cars/Nets4Trains/Nets4Aircraft 2014, LNCS 8435, pp. 23–29, 2014.

2   Standard IEEE 802.15.4 and Mobile Applications

The standard IEEE 802.15.4 was established in 2003 for wireless personal area networks. In the worldwide available frequency band of 2.4 GHz 16 different independent channels using DSSS (direct sequence spread spectrum) are available. According to European regulations [4] the maximum allowed radiated power is 10 mW per MHz and will be up to 20 dBm since 2015. Most devices are designed for radiation power of ~0 dBm especially in residential and commercial applications due to the energy consumption. Main applications can be found on home automation, industrial control and consumer electronics. The gross data rate is 250 kBps.

Many applications and performance analyses have been done to improve the standard's behavior in simulations and in hardware tests (e.g. [8], [9]). Also approaches for applications of IEEE 802.15.4 based systems in cars were done since years (e.g. [10], [11]). Only few applications of WSNs inside a car or other moving system were realized [12], [13].

3   TEDRA Test Equipment

The TEDRA System [5] shown in Fig.1 (Thermo Couple Enhanced Disk Brake Radio Access) is a flexible and easy mountable system to transmit wireless the temperatures of the disk brake to the on board receiver.

Fig. 1. TEDRA System with 4 transmitters and one receiver

The TEDRA System is fully compliant to the IEEE 802.15.4 standard. Its transmission power of each component is up to 10 dBm. The PAN-coordinator observes each transmission from and to each associated node. Therefore any

Fig. 2. Test vehicle with mounted sensor nodes on the rim

transmission problem can be detected immediately. Also each node itself observes its transmission towards the coordinator. Here also any transmission problem can be detected immediately. Each sensor node is mounted on the rim during test drives as shown in Fig. 2.

The TEDRA System was one of the first IEEE 802.15.4 based wireless systems for automotive test and measurement applications on the market.

4   Frequency Agility and Channel Selection

One common use case of IEEE 802.15.4 is called frequency agility. The network starts an energy detection scan if any interference is detected to analyze the actual RF environment. Afterwards the network rebuilds itself using a clean channel. The duration of a complete energy detection scan throughout all 16 channels starts at 492 ms and can take up to 134 min [1].

4.1   Standard Channel Selection

After each passive scan the operation channel has to be chosen. The standard algorithm for e.g. Freescale based IEEE 802.15.4 platforms works as following [7]:

For each channel a value for the measured signal power is determined. This value of the first channel will be compared with the one of the second one and the one with lower signal power value will be chosen. The result will be compared to the third channel and again the one with lower signal power value will be chosen. If two values are equal, the first one will be chosen. After comparing all 16 channels of the 2.4 GHz band the first one with the smallest value will be the resulting one.

4.2   Intelligent Channel Selection

The Intelligent Channel Selection takes notice of the actual used channel and a fast ED scan was started. If a certain signal power is identified, this channel will not be taken into account anymore. The uncertainty of the measured values will be compensated by the selection algorithm. Each channel with the lowest value will get a weighting factor. This factor rises with the frequency distance to the actual used channel. Those 'weighted channels' are normalized to the sum of all. Afterwards a random access will chose one of the available channels. According to the weighting factor a channel of the opposite end has higher probability to be chosen. The old channel cannot be chosen anymore. This intelligent channel selection starts only if a transmission failure was detected [6]. After ~500 ms a new channel is selected as fig. 3 shows.

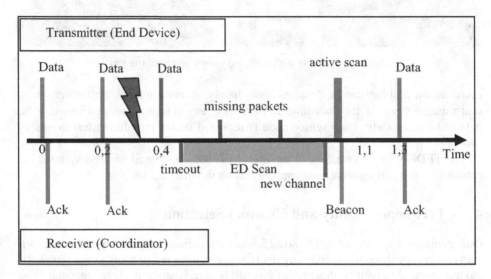

Fig. 3. Timing of intelligent channel selection with 200 ms transmission interval

5   Predictable Frequency Agility

For sensor networks with fast (e.g. 100 ms interval) and high dynamic measurement application much faster solutions are necessary. Wi-Fi as well as UMTS can be named as main interferences which disturb IEEE 802.15.4 transmissions. It is important to know that both technologies are showing a wide band behavior of ~4 to 8 channels towards the IEEE 802.15.4 standard. Fig. 4 shows typical Wi-Fi (blue) and IEEE 802.15.4 (red) spectral distributions as well as spurious emissions of UMTS (green) which can be found near base stations.

Also the different radiation power of usual 0 dBm devices and high power +10 dBm WSN devices are marked right in between the typical Wi-Fi channels.

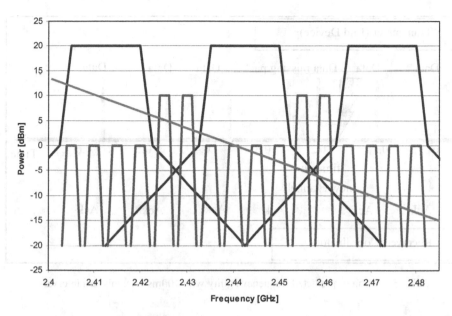

Fig. 4. Typical spectrum distribution with Wi-Fi, IEEE 802.15.4 and spurious emissions of WLAN

With certain uncertainness it can be predicted that the neighbor channel will also be affected by the external interference and a channel which is more than 8 channels apart will not be affected. Therefore each node can calculate itself the obviously clean channel out of the actual disturbed channel without any energy detection scan. Now a 'quasi synchronal channel change' is possible. This channel hop only starts if any interference occurs which cannot be corrected by several repetitions of the packet after a few milliseconds.

5.1   Method of Operation

Fig. 5 shows the fast behavior of predictable frequency agility. Here only one missing packet can be achieved if the calculated channel shows clean behavior. Due to the same calculation rules each node can follow in the same way – with immolating one missing packet. It can be parameterized what will happen in case of the new calculated channel is unsuitable for data transmission. A new channel will be calculated again out of the first one with interferences and the second one with interferences or a standard energy detection scan can start to listen into the RF environment.

Practical examinations show that maximum 3 channel switches should be enough to synchronize again the network. If this still fails an energy detection scan has to be made to actualize the RF environment.

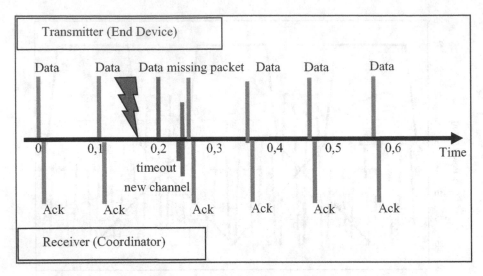

Fig. 5. Timing of predicted frequency agility with 100ms transmission interval

5.2   Advantages and Disadvantages

Compared to technologies which use frequency hopping based on IEEE 802.15.4 systems a much higher battery lifetime can be archived under harsh RF environments with changing conditions. Only in case of transmission problems the predicted frequency agility will start.

The tests show clearly that modern urban environments have the highest density of wireless communication which induces to transmission problems. While driving through the urban centers up to 12 channel hops can be realized during one minute.

Unfortunately there are still failed packets necessary to start the routine. 100% reliability can never be achieved even in areas with only few disturbing interferences.

6   Conclusions

The TEDRA System which transmits disk brake temperature data from the wheel to the on board unit uses now predicted frequency agility to improve best possible reliability in fast changing disturbing RF environmental conditions. With such a flexible technology IEEE 802.15.4 based systems can work in mobile applications with the advantage of minimal energy consumption and maximal battery lifetime. Especially for fast applications predicted frequency agility is a suitable solution to increase reliability of cheap and energy efficient transmission systems.

Redundant transmission in multiple channels or even multiple wireless frequency bands will offer best possible reliability, paid by higher energy consumption. If this is not possible, predicted frequency agility shows a very efficiency and fast solution for fast changing disturbing RF environment. It is not necessary to predict more than 3 channel switches as long as the network is not able to re-synchronize again. Then an actualization of the RF environment has to be done by an energy detection scan.

References

[1] http://www.ieee802.org/15/pub/TG4.html
[2] http://www.zigbee.org
[3] http://www.hartcomm.org/protocol/wihart/wireless_technology.html
[4] http://www.etsi.org (ETSI EN 300 328 V1.7.1 until 2014 and ETSI EN 300 328 V1.8.1 from 2015)
[5] http://www.senTec-Elektronik.de
[6] Binhack, M., Kupris, G.: Intelligent Channel Selection for IEEE 802.15.4 Rapid Applications. In: Proceedings Wireless Congress, Munich (2010)
[7] http://www.freescale.com/beekit
[8] Xia, F., Vinel, A., et al.: Evaluating IEEE 802.15.4 for Cyber-Physical Systems. EURASIP Journal on Wireless Communications and Networking, doi:10.1155/2011/596397
[9] Hildebrandt, H., Binhack, M.: Performance of different ZigBee enabled Hardware. In: Proceedings Embedded World Conference, Nuremberg (2006)
[10] Nolte, T., Hansson, H., Lo Bello, L.: Wireless Automotive Communications. In: Euromicro Conference on Real-Time Systems, Palma de Mallorca, vol. 6, pp. 35–38 (2005)
[11] Nolte, T., Hansson, H., Lo Bello, L.: Automotive Communicaions - Past, Current and Future. In: IEEE Conference on Emerging Technologies and Factory Automation (ETFA), vol. 1. IEEE (2005)
[12] Luo, C.: Automotive Tire Monitoring and Warning System Based on ZigBee Wireless Network. Advanced Engineering Forum 4, 27–31 (2012), doi:10.4028/www.scientific.net/AEF.4.27
[13] Broska, M., Binhack, M.: Disk Brake Temperature Measurement System with IEEE 802.15.4. In: Proceedings Wireless Congress, Munich (2009)

Context-Aware Retransmission Scheme for Increased Reliability in Platooning Applications

Annette Böhm, Magnus Jonsson, Kristina Kunert, and Alexey Vinel

CERES (Centre for Research on Embedded Systems)
Halmstad University, Halmstad, Sweden
{Annette.Bohm,Magnus.Jonsson,Kristina.Kunert,
Alexey.Vinel}@hh.se

Abstract. Recent advances in cooperative driving hold the potential to significantly improve safety, comfort and efficiency on our roads. An application of particular interest is platooning of vehicles, where reduced inter-vehicle gaps lead to considerable reductions in fuel consumption. This, however, puts high requirements on timeliness and reliability of the underlying exchange of control data. Considering the difficult radio environment and potentially long distances between communicating platoon members, as well as the random channel access method used by the IEEE 802.11p standard for short-range inter-vehicle communication, those requirements are very difficult to meet. The relatively static topology of a platoon, however, enables us to preschedule communication within the platoon over a dedicated service channel. Furthermore, we are able to set aside parts of the available bandwidth for retransmission of packets in order to fulfil the reliability requirements stated by the platoon control application. In this paper, we describe the platooning framework along with the scheduling algorithm used to assign retransmission slots to control packets that are most likely to need them. This retransmission scheduling scheme offers a valuable tool for system designers when answering questions about the number of safely supported vehicles in a platoon, achievable reductions in inter-vehicle gaps and periodicity of control packets.

Keywords: Platooning, cooperative driving, VANETs, real-time communication, vehicular communication, retransmission scheme, scheduling.

1 Introduction

Cooperative driving holds the potential of revolutionizing the way we travel on our roads today. With the exchange of status information and occasional warning messages between vehicles, a vehicle is no longer limited to its own sensor readings but is able to assess the current traffic situation within a radius of several hundred meters. This information is the foundation of a large variety of future cooperative driving applications targeting enhanced safety, efficiency and comfort on our roads. The feasibility and success of such applications rely entirely on the performance of the underlying communication network with fast and reliable information exchange

A. Sikora et al. (Eds.): Nets4Cars/Nets4Trains/Nets4Aircraft 2014, LNCS 8435, pp. 30–42, 2014.

over an unreliable wireless communication channel as a prerequisite. The timely and reliable treatment of safety-critical data is further complicated by the communication protocol choices made for the recently adopted IEEE 802.11p standard [1] for short-range vehicular ad-hoc networks (VANETs), coupled with the European requirement to use one common 10 MHz control channel (CC) shared by both periodic status updates and event-triggered warning messages. In terms of Medium Access Control (MAC), IEEE 802.11p uses a decentralized random access protocol. A quality of service (QoS) differentiation of four priority classes for different message types is in place, whereas there is no mechanism to individually treat vehicles depending on their importance to the application or the current radio conditions at hand. Furthermore, the standard assumes broadcast to be the only communication model required in VANET applications. Acknowledgements are not feasible and therefore retransmissions of not successfully received packets are not considered, which considerably decreases the reliability and real-time properties of the standard compliant communication network. In order to fulfil the strict requirements of future safety-critical cooperative driving, application-specific and context-aware adaptations to the standard are needed. In this paper, we therefore propose and evaluate a context-aware retransmission scheme for time-critical status information exchange in a platooning application.

Platooning can be seen as the first step towards the realization of fully autonomous driving. Vehicles join a platoon lead by a designated driver and follow this leading vehicle with a minimal inter-vehicle spacing. A reduction in fuel consumption of 14% has been reported for a three-truck platoon with a 10 m gap between the trucks [2], while even higher savings are possible with shorter gaps. In practice, however, platooning requires an automated control loop to be constantly fed with up-to-date information about the status of each platoon member in order to be able to quickly adapt to changes and maintain safety. The basic status update messages used by the standard (defined as Cooperative Awareness Messages (CAM) in Europe and Basic Status Messages (BSM) in North America) include information about a vehicle's position, speed and driving direction. Due to the particularly strict requirements on status exchange within a platoon, we argue that simple periodic broadcast on the common control channel (shared with other vehicles within the platoon's radio range) is not a viable option. We therefore suggest the use of a dedicated service channel (SC) for intra-platoon communication only. Furthermore, compared to other VANET applications, platoons constitute a relatively static network topology where changes only happen in the comparably rare situation of a vehicle leaving or a new one joining the platoon.

In this paper, we present an analysis tool for the context-aware distribution of communication resources between platoon members. The goal is to improve the timing and reliability properties of periodic control data spread within the platoon for safety and maintenance purposes. This is done by introducing a retransmission phase shared by all real-time channels, i.e., all sender-receiver pairs with application defined timing and reliability requirements. This retransmission phase is divided into time slots and slots are assigned to real-time channels depending on their probability of successful packet reception. In other words, a packet to a far destination (and thereby with a lower probability to be successfully received) will receive more retransmission opportunities than a packet to a close destination. With this context-aware resource assignment the target packet reception probability required by the platoon control application is more likely to be met.

The rest of the paper is organized as follows: Chapter 2 provides a background to relevant aspects of the current standard and discusses related works. In Chapters 3 and 4, we introduce the system assumptions and provide details of the protocol framework, respectively. The scheduling optimization and evaluation are presented in Chapter 5, while Chapter 6 concludes this paper.

2   Background and Related Works

The amendment IEEE 802.11p [1] defines physical and MAC layer details for short to medium range communication in a VANET. ETSI has standardized a profile of IEEE 802.11p adapted to the 30 MHz frequency spectrum at the 5.9 GHz band allocated in Europe [3] and considers two types of messages, periodic status updates, CAMs [4] and event-triggered warning messages, DENMs [5]. One dedicated control channel is reserved for data exchange in traffic-safety applications and shared between CAMs and DENMs. Additionally, service channels are available and can, e.g., be used for certain applications as platooning as long as mandatory listening periods to the control channel are kept. Alternatively, a second transceiver pair needs to be installed and tuned to the service channel (as employed for a platooning scenario in [6]), while the primary transceiver pair stays tuned to the control channel.

The MAC layer of IEEE 802.11p uses CSMA/CA, where a node attempts to transmit only if the channel is sensed free during a certain time period (Arbitration Inter Frame Spacing, AIFS). If the channel is busy or if it becomes busy during the AIFS, the node randomizes a back-off time, which is counted down only during time periods when the channel is sensed free. When the back-off value reaches zero, the node transmits directly without any further delay. This random access protocol introduces unbounded delays, especially at high node density or high data loads as can be found in platoon control applications with its demand for frequent status updates. Slot-based, time division multiple access (TDMA) protocols have therefore been proposed for VANETs. In [7], the self-organizing TDMA protocol is adapted to a vehicular scenario, successfully providing guaranteed access to all nodes through distance-based slot reuse. [6] successfully uses a slotted, prescheduled approach for CAM exchange, making use of the predictability of the bandwidth needs of periodic status updates in a platooning scenario.

Timing and reliability issues in VANETs have been subject to many studies, where either channel access alone [6], [7] is targeted, or channel access in combination with retransmission schemes [8], [9]. Since the IEEE 802.11p standard assumes simple broadcast, no acknowledgements are used and thereby no collision detection is possible. Many papers concerned with improved reliability in VANETs disregard this fact and introduce acknowledgements to keep the sender informed about the success of a transmission. In a broadcast environment, this knowledge can even be used by other vehicles in the reception range of a packet to determine the best candidate to relay a packet without wasting valuable bandwidth by causing a broadcast storm [8] [9] [10]. As we assume every platoon member to be in each other's transmission range, multihop communication is not our concern and retransmissions are merely used to increase the probability of successful packet reception within the one-hop neighbourhood. Acknowledgements are bandwidth intensive. Acknowledging each broadcast packet, as, e.g., described in [10], introduces unnecessary overhead where the bandwidth should rather be used for data transmissions. In [11], Shafiq et al. design a block acknowledgement scheme for VANET broadcasts to reduce this overhead. We argue that the rather predictable link quality between sender and receiver pairs in a platoon make acknowledgements redundant. Boukerche et al. [12] describe a protocol to estimate the reliability of unicast links in a VANET and use that knowledge to group those links into QoS classes. As in our work, no acknowledgements are needed to achieve this classification. Boukerche et al. do however not make use of retransmissions to boost the success ratio of packets over a certain link.

While our proposed retransmission algorithm attempts to improve the packet reception probability through unicast retransmissions based on channel estimation, other studies are concerned with enhanced reliability by making the first transmission more likely to succeed. The authors of [13], e.g., look at the effect of transmit power and contention window adaptations to achieve a higher packet reception probability. Even [14] studies the correlation between reliability and transmission range in VANETs. Neither of those works takes their results one step further and studies further improvements to reliability through retransmission of the packet. In earlier work, [15], we designed a communication and real-time analysis framework over a dedicated frequency channel for platoon applications and show that our retransmission scheme is able to decrease the message error rate of control data exchange within a platoon. In the current work, we make a step further and propose an adaptive retransmission scheme, which explicitly takes into account different links qualities between platoon members.

3   System Assumptions

The special circumstances and prerequisites of platooning set this application apart from other less static and predictable VANET applications and enable us to make a number of choices that deviate from the specifications found in, e.g., the IEEE 802.11p standard.

1. We assume the presence of a dedicated service channel used for intra-platoon communication only, while a second transceiver is tuned to the common control channel shared with any other vehicles and VANET applications for the transmission of non-platoon specific CAMs, DENMs and service announcements as required by the standard. This separation of communication within the platoon and with surrounding vehicles has two important advantages. Firstly, the bandwidth of the platooning service channel is not shared with data from non-platoon vehicles with potentially lower timing and reliability requirements.

Secondly, by keeping intra-platoon communication separate from other VANET applications, we can make use of the comparably static topology of a platoon in the design of pre-scheduled, deterministic MAC and retransmission schemes.

2. Platoon members are assigned different roles, depending on their position within the platoon. The first vehicle, called platoon leader, has special responsibilities when it comes to the maintenance and control of the platoon, while all other vehicles, regular vehicles, merely follow. We assume that the platoon leader makes general control decisions concerning the entire platoon, while regular vehicles are simply required to maintain a constant gap to the vehicle in front and follow orders from the leader. This model requires that the entire platoon is within the leader's transmission range, restricting the feasible length of a platoon. The integration of longer platoons in the proposed retransmission scheme would require multihop communication, an aspect left as future work for now.

3. A platoon is maintained by an automated control loop that needs to be continuously fed with current status information. It is a realistic assumption that the following data will be needed and combined to make this possible:

    a. There is still a need for CAMs and DENMs broadcasted on the common control channel as specified by the standard. This ensures that the platoon is well integrated into other VANET applications and that its members are "visible" to surrounding non-platoon vehicles. Furthermore, the status information in periodically broadcasted CAMs is still useful to the platooning application, even if the CAM report rate of 2 - 10 Hz and the reliability offered by the standard do not satisfy the requirements of the platoon control loop.

    b. In addition to the afore-mentioned CAMs on the control channel, platoon vehicles are assumed to send out CAM-like status updates even on the service channel. As communication on the service channel is not restricted to the message types and report rates stated by the standard, both the content and the periodicity of those status messages can be adapted to the control requirements of the platooning application. Furthermore, we are able to make use of the periodic nature of such status updates and preschedule them in a slot-based MAC protocol, considerably increasing the packets' real-time and reliability properties.

    c. A platoon vehicle's distance to its immediate neighbours (most importantly to the vehicle in front) is constantly assessed by the means of radar. Combined with the afore-mentioned CAMs from both the control channel and the service channel, this provides each vehicle with a sufficient understanding of its neighbourhood to adapt to minor changes in speed and maintain a constant inter-vehicle distance.

    d. The control of the platoon as a whole requires a more centralized approach where a designated vehicle (preferably the leading vehicle) makes control decisions for the entire platoon and distributes these to the platoon members on a regular basis. As those packets contain individual information to specific platoon members, we view them as unicast transmissions. In other words, while they can still be overheard by other vehicles in the radio range, those unicast packets have one specified destination. Due to their safety-critical content, it is vital that the unicast control packets reach their destination within a certain deadline and with a very high reception probability. This aspect is targeted by the retransmission protocol described below.

e. Unforeseen events might require the swift dissemination of warning messages within the platoon. Inter-vehicle gaps of merely a few meters put timing requirements on the warning dissemination that DENMs sent over the shared (and in emergency situations probably overloaded) control channel with its IEEE 802.11p random access MAC protocol will not be able to fulfil. We see, however, two ways of issuing event-triggered warning messages over the designated service channel. Firstly, a part of the bandwidth could be reserved for such kinds of spontaneous bursts of warning messages. During those event-based phases, no periodic control data transmissions are scheduled. Secondly, warning content could be integrated into the periodic control data transmissions (as described under c. above), i.e., hazard warnings would be spread inside control packets with the same real-time and reliability properties as guaranteed for control data. In the scope of this paper, we do not further explore the integration of event-based warnings into the platooning application.

4. Furthermore, we assume that every vehicle knows its position within the platoon. This information is provided by the control packets sent out by the platoon leader. The topology of a platoon is stable until a vehicle leaves the platoon or a new vehicle requests to join. A vehicle that wants to leave the platoon would have to announce this action to the leader who informs the concerned platoon members and instructs them to close the gap. In case a new vehicle requests to join, it has to make its intention known to the platoon leader (e.g. via communication on a control channel) and wait for instructions on its position within the platoon. (For fuel efficiency reasons, vehicles are expected to be sorted by size, which does not allow vehicles to simply join the end of the platoon.) Unicast messages to involved platoon members are used to organize this process.

Summarizing, we assume that the dedicated service channel is used by two message types enabling the control within a platoon: CAM-like status updates that are broadcasted periodically by every platoon member and unicast control packets issued by the platoon leader with individual vehicles as intended recipients. Due to the importance of the unicast control packets to the control loop of the platoon, this message type should be given the opportunity of retransmissions. Figure 1 explains the communication patterns considered.

4   Protocol Framework

We propose a collision-free slotted MAC protocol, where time is divided into superframes, SF, which in their turn are divided into time slots corresponding to the transmission time of one maximum-sized packet. A part of the SF is set aside for the retransmission of packets that are not fulfilling the packet reception probability requirement with only the regular transmission. The protocol framework in terms of SF design and retransmission scheduling is described below.

4.1 Superframe Design

We assume that a message never is longer than one packet and that both status updates and control packets are of comparable length, i.e., one time slot with duration T_{slot}. The first slot in the frame is used for a synchronization beacon transmitted by the platoon leader to all the members to announce the SF start. We divide the rest of a SF into three phases (see Figure 2):

a. The *collection phase*, where the broadcast of CAM-like status messages is done. This information benefits both the platoon members in their assessment of their immediate neighborhood and the platoon leader in its assessment of the overall platoon status. The duration of the collection phase, $T_{collection}$, corresponds to the current number of ordinary platoon members (denoted as N) plus the platoon leader itself, i.e., $T_{collection} = (N + 1) \cdot T_{slot}$.

b. The *control phase*, which is N slots long, is used by the platoon leader to send unicast control data to each of the other platoon members. The duration of the control phase is therefore $T_{control} = N \cdot T_{slot}$.

c. For increased reliability of the unicast control data, a third phase, the *retransmission phase*, $T_{retrans} = K \cdot T_{slot}$, is present. Depending on the assessed need for retransmissions, a number of retransmission slots, $\leq K$, are assigned to different communication channels, where a communication channel is defined by a unique sender-receiver pair. Details on the choice and assignment of retransmission slots, RT slots, are given in the following subsection.

4.2 Retransmission Scheduling

While the length of the collection and control phases is determined by the number of vehicles in the platoon, the length of the retransmission phase depends on one of the following factors (See Figure 3):

1. The update frequency (periodicity) of control data required by the application. As we assume the update frequency to be identical to the SF length, this parameter determines the maximum SF length and consequently the number of available RT slots.

2. The level of reliability required by the application. The platoon control loop specifies a minimum or target Packet Reception Probability (PRP) that needs to be achieved by the underlying communication network in order to safely maintain a platoon of a certain length and with certain inter-vehicle gaps.

Although both a target PRP and a required update period might be requested by the application, it will not always be possible to fulfil both requests. The number of required RT slots to maintain a certain target PRP might, e.g., not fit in the RT phase available for the specified SF length for the current number of platoon members. We assume that, in most scenarios, the periodicity of control data is the fixed parameter. In that case, the requirements on the target PRP have to be relaxed, meaning that the safety of the platoon travelling with the current inter-vehicle gaps cannot be sufficiently supported any more, but that inter-vehicle gaps might have to be increased. Alternatively, the number of vehicles in the platoon has to be reduced to free more slots within the SF for retransmissions.

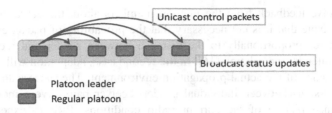

Fig. 1. Communication Pattern

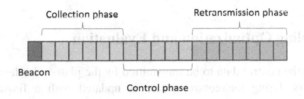

Fig. 2. Superframe Format

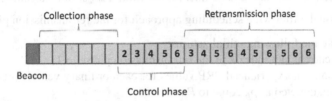

Fig. 3. Retransmission Phase Example

The PRP, P_i, $1 \leq i \leq N$, of packets from the leader to the i-th ordinary member depends on, e.g., the distance between them as well as the number and size of the intermediate vehicles (trucks or cars). Studies [16] have shown that the number of intermediate vehicles, blocking the line-of-sight path between sender and receiver, obviously plays an important role to the channel quality. Depending on the PRP for a particular member, unicast transmission to it is in more or less need of retransmissions. The number and actual assignment of slots needed in the retransmission phase depends on the current PRP values P_i on the platooning service channel. Members that are expected to suffer from more frequent packet loss should receive a higher number of retransmission attempts (i.e., assigned RT slots) than those who experience better channel conditions. This requires knowledge at the leader side of the currently achievable PRP for all the members for the assignment of slots in the RT phase.

The PRP values P_i used by the leader for the scheduling can be either computed beforehand using any model reflecting the configuration of the platoon or adapted during the operation by utilizing the estimations of current P_i values by the leader. In the first case, the scheduling is able to catch major propagation differences between the members caused by the different sizes and positions of the vehicles. This rather static assessment of the expected PRP is purely based on predetermined models and does not involve feedback from the platoon members about the actual experienced PRP at hand. Note that it is not necessary that the probability of packet errors in the platoon increases proportionally to the distance between sender and receiver even though there often is a correlation [16]. In the second case, adaptation will also tend to catch the influence of the actual propagation environment. The success and failure of recent transmissions between individual sender-receiver pairs give a more accurate and fine-grained picture of the current radio conditions. PRP P_i experienced by member i is included in the payload of the packet it broadcasts during the collection phase.

5   Scheduling Optimization and Evaluation

We assume that the control data to be transmitted by the platoon leader to each of the platoon members during the control phase is updated with a fixed interval not exceeding the application requirement T_{update}^{max}. The SF duration coincides with the actually chosen control data update interval duration, T_{update}, not exceeding T_{update}^{max}.

We propose the following scheduling approach for the retransmission phase:

Step 0. Make the following initializations:
- Set current slot index k in the retransmission phase to 1;
- Set current experienced PRP values for each ordinary vehicle (out of total N) in SF, denoted as p_i, equal to P_i;
- Set the current number of transmission attempts M_i for each ordinary vehicle to 1.

Step 1. Choose the vehicle with index j, which has the lowest p_j value and schedule it for retransmission in slot k.

Step 2. Increment M_j. Assign $1 - (1 - P_j)^{M_j}$ as new value for p_j.

Step 3. If there are more retransmissions to schedule, i.e., $k < K$, then increment k and go to Step 1, otherwise stop.

The PRP per SF achieved for a given number of vehicles in the platoon $N+1$ and a fixed control data update interval duration T_{update} can be computed as $P_{actual} = \min p_j$. If the requirement on a target PRP P_{target} is imposed, then the minimal SF duration $T_{update} \leq T_{update}^{max}$, allowing to meet P_{target}, can be determined as follows.

Let $q_i^{(M)} = 1 - (1 - P_i)^M$ be the probability that the leader requires not more than M attempts for the successful delivery to the i-th member of the platoon (in other words this is the probability that at least one of M attempts of the leader is successful). Then $M_{min}^{(i)} = \arg\min_{q_i^{(M_i)} \geq P_{target}} q_i^{(M_i)}$ is the minimum number of transmission attempts that should be done by the leader for the i-th ordinary platoon member in order to provide the target PRP.

Therefore, the required SF duration is

$$T_{update} = \left(2 + N + \sum_{i=1}^{N} M_{min}^{(i)} \right) T_{slot} \leq T_{update}^{max}$$

where $2 + N$ signifies one synchronization slot plus the collection phase.

Above, we presented the scheduling algorithm for RT slots in a SF of predefined length. We thereby provide a scheduling tool where the required control update frequency is coupled to the supported platoon length and the achievable PRP. Figures 4 and 5 visualize that connection. The parameters used are a bit rate of 6 Mbps and a data packet length of 400 bytes, corresponding to a packet duration of 642 µs. In order to account for a deterioration of the channel quality due to fading and shadowing (by vehicles situated in-between sender and receiver), the simulated PRP is reduced by 5 percentage points for every intermediate vehicle. PRP is therefore calculated as PRP $= 1 - (N_{hop} \times 0.05)$, where $N_{hop} = 1$ if the sending and receiving vehicles are direct neighbours, $N_{hop} = 2$ if there is one vehicle in-between, etc.

According to earlier measurement campaigns [17], testing the achievable transmission range of IEEE 802.11p-enabled communication equipment, radio ranges beyond 500 m are not realistic, not even when considering direct line-of-sight (LOS) communication. Assuming an antenna-to-antenna spacing of 30 m, i.e., considering two trucks following each other, we therefore restrict the number of platoon members in our evaluation to 15, including the platoon leader.

In Figure 4 the packet reception ratio is plotted as a function of the platoon length, including the leading vehicle, for five different fixed SF durations. The SF durations simulated are 20 ms, 25 ms, 40 ms, 50 ms, and 100 ms. A SF duration of 20 ms will only provide the possibility of one retransmission attempt for a platoon length of 15 vehicles. This also means that SF durations shorter than 20 ms will not support 15 vehicles at all as not each vehicle will get a time slot for its ordinary transmission. Assuming a SF duration of 20 ms, a packet reception ratio of almost 1, i.e., almost no errors at all, can be achieved for a platoon length up to 7 vehicles. For 10 vehicles the packet reception ratio is still over 0.9, but for longer platoon sizes, the success rate decreases quickly. For the maximum platoon length supported, the reception rate is down to only 0.35. Increasing the SF duration by merely 5 ms to 25 ms will increase the packet reception ratio for the 15-vehicle platoon to 0.6, and to reach over 0.9, the platoon cannot be longer than 11 vehicles. For the three longest simulated SF durations, the packet reception rate never dropped under the 0.9 mark, and a 100 ms SF will result in nearly error free performance.

In Figure 5, the minimum SF duration as a function of the platoon length is plotted instead. Curves are given for different fixed target PRPs. The target PRPs simulated are 0.9, 0.99, 0.999 and 0.9999. As seen in the figure, the curves for the different target PRP values behave in a similar way. For the lowest PRP studied, 0.9, a maximum-sized platoon (15 vehicles) will need a SF duration of about 40 ms. The increase of the target PRP by one order of magnitude will add approximately 25 ms of SF duration, leading to a SF duration of about 120 ms for the highest target PRP of 0.9999.

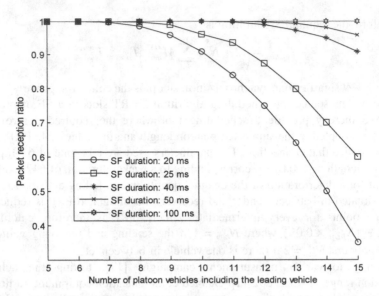

Fig. 4. PRP for various SF lengths and platoon sizes

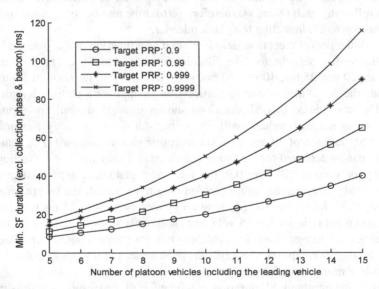

Fig. 5. Achievable SF length for various target PRPs and platoon sizes

According to our assumptions, the SF duration and the update rate of the application are identical, meaning that a longer SF would correspond to a lower update frequency. A more detailed study of a higher update rate versus more retransmission possibilities is, however, outside the scope of this paper, and left as on-going future work.

6   Conclusion

In this paper, we presented a communication framework and retransmission scheme for increased reliability of safety-critical control data transmissions in a platooning application. In order to provide the necessary update rate of status and control messages to maintain a platoon of heavy vehicles at inter-vehicle gaps of 10 meters or less, a target packet reception probability should be met even for sender-receiver pairs that are several hundred meters apart, with a potentially high number of intermediate vehicles deteriorating the signal quality. Our framework set aside a part of the available bandwidth for retransmissions of packets that can be assumed to experience packet errors. The lower the expected packet reception probability of a unicast link, the more retransmission slots are assigned to that link by the proposed retransmission scheduling algorithm. Our framework provides a tool that balances reliability requirements (a requested probability of packet reception), update frequency of periodic control messages and the number of vehicles and their inter-vehicle gap that can safely be supported in the platoon. This is done based on an estimation of the link quality, a value that is expected to remain fairly stable due to the stable topology found in a platoon. As no acknowledgements are needed, no additional overhead is added besides the bandwidth used for scheduled retransmissions.

References

1. IEEE Std. 802.11-2012 Part11: Wireless LAN Medium Access Control (MAC) and Physical Layer (PHY) specifications (March 2012)
2. Tsugawa, S., Kato, S., Aoki, K.: An automated truck platoon for energy saving. In: 2011 IEEE/RSJ International Conference on Intelligent Robots and Systems, San Francisco, CA, USA, September 25–30, pp. 4109–4114 (2011)
3. ETSI EN 302 663: Draft V1.3.2, ITS; Access Layer Specification for Intelligent Transport Systems operating in the 5 GHz frequency band, Tech. Rep. (2010)
4. ETSI EN 637-2: ITS; Vehicular Communications; Basic Set of Applications; Part 2: Specification of Cooperative Awareness Basic Service (June 2012)
5. ETSI EN 637-3: ITS; Vehicular Communications; Basic Set of Applications; Part 2: Specification of Decentralized Environmental Notification Basic Service (June 2012)
6. Böhm, A., Jonsson, M., Uhlemann, E.: Performance evaluation of a platooning application using IEEE 802.11p on a control channel vs. a centralized real-time MAC on a service channel. In: Proc. IEEE Int. Conf. on Wireless and Mobile Computing, Networking and Communications (WiMob), Lyon, France, pp. 545–552 (October 2013)
7. Bilstrup, K., Uhlemann, E., Ström, E.G., Bilstrup, U.: On the Ability of the 802.11p MAC Method and STDMA to Support Real-Time Vehicle-to-Vehicle Communications. EURASIP J. on Wireless Communication and Networking, 1–14 (2009)
8. Omar, H.A., Zhuang, W., Li, L.: VeMAC: A TDMA-Based MAC Protocol for Reliable Broadcast in VANETs. IEEE Trans. on Mobile Computing, 1724–1736 (September 2013)
9. Borgonovo, F., Capone, A., Cesana, M., Fratta, L.: ADHOC MAC: a new MAC Architecture for ad hoc Networks Providing Efficient and Reliable Point-to-Point and Broadcast Services. In: Wireless Networks (WINET), vol. 10(4), pp. 359–366 (July 2004)

10. Zhen, X., Wang, J., Wang, P., Wang, X., Liu, F.: A Sender-Initiated Adaptive and Reliable Broadcast Scheme for VANET Safety Message. In: Proc. Intern., Symposium on Information Science and Engineering (ISISE), Shanghai, China, December 14-16, pp. 329–334 (2012)

11. Shafiq, Z., Mahmud, S.A., Khan, G.M., Zafar, H., Al-Raweshidy, H.S.: A Complete Transmission Acknowledgement Scheme for VANETs. In: Proc. 13th International Conference on ITS Telecommunications (ITST), Tampere, Finland, pp. 238–243 (November 2013)

12. Boukerche, A., Rezende, C., Pazzi, R.W.: A Link-Reliability-Based Approach to Providing QoS Support for VANETs. In: Proc. IEEE International Conference on Communications (ICC), Dresden, Germany, pp. 1–5 (June 2009)

13. Rawat, D.B., Popescu, D.C., Gongjun Yan, Y., Olariu, S.: Enhancing VANET Performance by Joint Adaptation of Transmission Power and Contention Window Size. IEEE Transactions on Parallel and Distributed Systems 22(9), 1528–1535 (2011)

14. Hongsheng, L., Poellabauer, C.: Balancing broadcast reliability and transmission range in VANETs. In: Proc. IEEE Veh. Netw. Conf., Jersey City, NJ, USA, pp. 247–254 (December 2010)

15. Jonsson, M., Kunert, K., Böhm, A.: Increased communication reliability for delay-sensitive platooning applications on top of IEEE 802.11p. In: Berbineau, M., et al. (eds.) Nets4Cars/Nets4Trains 2013. LNCS, vol. 7865, pp. 121–135. Springer, Heidelberg (2013)

16. Bergenhem, C., Coelingh, E., Johansson, R., Soltani-Tehrani, A.: V2V communication quality: measurements in a cooperative automotive platooning application. In: SAE 2014 World Congress, Detroit, MI, USA, April 8-10 (2014)

17. Böhm, A., Lidström, K., Jonsson, M., Larsson, T.: Evaluating CALM M5-based vehicle-to-vehicle communication in various road settings through field trials. In: Proc. IEEE LCN Workshop on User Mobility and Vehicular Netw., Denver, CO, pp. 613–620 (October 2010)

An Improved Relevance Estimation Function for Cooperative Awareness Messages in VANETs

Jakob Breu[1,2] and Michael Menth[2]

[1] Daimler AG, Sindelfingen, Germany
jakob.breu@daimler.com
[2] University of Tübingen, Tübingen, Germany
menth@uni-tuebingen.de

Abstract. According to the current status of European Vehicular Ad-Hoc Network (VANET) standardization, vehicles gather and process Cooperative Awareness Messages (CAMs) sent from their environment. The rate of CAMs received by each vehicle can be high, and due to limited resources in series vehicles their processing is an open challenge. Following previous work, we present an improved relevance estimation function which calculates a relevance value for each received message based on basic information like position, speed, and heading without map data. Other than before, the new function incorporates non-static movement extrapolation of vehicles. We evaluate the newly proposed function using a receiver-centric approach.

1 Introduction

Wireless communication between vehicles and road side infrastructure is one of the key technologies to increase road traffic safety, to enable more comfortable driving, and to improve ecological and economic efficiency of road traffic [1]. The industry, research institutes, and the public sector made great efforts to develop technologies and standards for such systems. The most common terms for these efforts are *Vehicular Ad-Hoc Networks* (VANETs), *Vehicle-to-Vehicle Communication* (V2V), or *Car-to-Car-Communication* (Car2Car, C2C).

After years of research and standardization, VANET technology is on the leap to market introduction [2]. National and international field tests demonstrate the feasibility of the elaborated standards [3]. In Europe VANETs are mainly based on two message types: status information messages and event-based messages [4][5]. While the latter are sent rarely on detection of specific events, status information messages are frequently sent to give their receivers the possibility to maintain a local dynamic map of their surrounding vehicles. Based on this information various applications can be implemented which need access to the knowledge of the current traffic situation.

The standards for VANETs focus on the interoperability between vehicles from all car manufacturers and hardware from different suppliers. Hence, the message transmission on the wireless channel is well studied. In contrast, the

A. Sikora et al. (Eds.): Nets4Cars/Nets4Trains/Nets4Aircraft 2014, LNCS 8435, pp. 43–56, 2014.

processing of status messages inside the receiving cars requires more investigation. The implementations in field tests either utilized powerful hardware or had to handle only few communicating vehicles. In series vehicle systems, the hardware is embedded and less powerful than in research systems. Also, the number of participating vehicles will increase steadily in the coming years [6]. Therefore, each equipped series vehicle must be able to cope with a rising penetration rate of VANET technology in vehicular traffic. However, this goal must be reached with a small-sized embedded VANET implementation for the entire lifetime of the vehicle [7]. Assuming the wireless channel and the network stack to be sized appropriately, the handling and processing of received messages remains a challenge.

Our approach to this problem is to estimate the relevance of messages on arrival and to process most relevant messages first. In case of overload in the receiving vehicle, least relevant messages are dropped or processed late. A particular difficulty of that approach is the relevance estimation. It should not rely on map information because map matching is considered an expensive operation.

A general assumption is that the relevance of messages from nearby senders is higher than from distant senders. However, vehicles are moving so that they could come closer within short time, which would also result in relatively high relevance values. In previous work [8] we have proposed a simple relevance estimation function that maximizes the relevance value of a message by extrapolating the position of the sender based on static movement, without changes in speed and heading. This work extends that approach by considering the sending vehicle may brake, accelerate, or drive curves to maximize the relevance value.

The remainder of this paper is organized as follows. Section 2 briefly reviews related work, introduces the Cooperative Awareness Message type, and summarizes our earlier work about a simple relevance estimation function. In Section 3 we derive an improved relevance function in several steps. We illustrate the effects of that function under various conditions in Section 4. Finally, Section 5 concludes this work and gives an outlook on further research.

2   Related Work

We first give a brief overview of field operational tests of VANETs. Then, we introduce Cooperative Awareness Messages (CAMs) and summarize our study of future CAM rates that series vehicles are likely to be faced with. Moreover, we give an introduction to the simple relevance estimation function we proposed in previous work. Furthermore, we delimit our work from research in the field of automotive situation assessment.

2.1   Field Operational Tests

Standards for VANET technologies are currently finalized, and field operational tests are conducted to investigate their interoperability and feasibility. In this context there are three big field operational tests in Europe: sim^{TD} (Germany), score@F (France) and DRIVE C2X (international) [9][10][11]. All of these tests utilize powerful hardware which cannot be used for series vehicles because of special automotive requirements regarding robustness, size, and cost.

2.2 Cooperative Awareness Messages

All vehicles in a VANET should be able to track their surrounding traffic situation. To facilitate this, vehicles and certain road side stations sends status messages on a regular basis. They are called Cooperative Awareness Messages (CAMs) and contain information like message identifier, station type, position, heading, speed, acceleration, and more. Upon reception and interpretation of CAMs the receiver can create a local dynamic map (LDM). CAMs are triggered when the heading, position or speed of a vehicle changes by more than given thresholds. The CAM send frequency lies between 1 and 10 Hz [5].

2.3 Analysis of CAM Rates

In an earlier work we analyzed the rates of CAMs in typical highway scenarios [12]. We used a new statistical channel model based on the Nakagami m-distribution for signal attenuation. Our simulations resulted in rates of 500 $\frac{\text{CAMs}}{\text{s}}$ which are received by vehicles in the presence of a VANET penetration rate of 40% and an uncongested channel. This gives an order of magnitude for the processing requirements in series vehicles.

2.4 Simple Relevance Estimation Function

In previous work [8] we presented a simple relevance estimation function for collision related VANET applications. Given basic information (positions, headings, speeds) about the sender α and receiver β of the message, the function calculates a relevance value $R(\alpha, \beta)$ by

$$R(\alpha, \beta) = \max_{t_{\text{now}} \leq t \leq t_{\text{now}} + T_{\text{max}}} \left[\frac{m}{\max(d(\alpha, \beta, t), d_{\text{min}})} \cdot \left(1 + \frac{t - t_{\text{now}}}{s} \right)^{-\gamma} \right] \quad (1)$$

with starting time t_{now}, extrapolation duration T_{max} (D_{max} in [8]), minimum distance d_{min} and time penalty exponent γ [8]. Distances are given in meters and time is given in seconds. The term $d(\alpha, \beta, t)$ denotes the straight-line distance between sender and receiver at time t and can be computed by

$$d(\alpha, \beta, t) = |\mathbf{p}_\beta + (t - t_{\text{now}}) \cdot \mathbf{v}_\beta - (\mathbf{p}_\alpha + (t - t_{\text{now}}) \cdot \mathbf{v}_\alpha)| \quad (2)$$

with position vectors $\mathbf{p}_\alpha$, $\mathbf{p}_\beta$ and constant velocity vectors $\mathbf{v}_\alpha$, $\mathbf{v}_\beta$ for sender and receiver, respectively. The maximization of the expression in brackets essentially means that the relevance of a message can be also high if its sender approaches the receiver only over time. The relevance function $R(\alpha, \beta)$ can be calculated efficiently for each received CAM [8].

However, it has some limitations that result from the assumption of static movement along the initial direction with constant speed. As a consequence, the relevance of distant senders is too much dominated by their headings. If they point towards the receiver, their static movement will bring them eventually very close to the receiver leading to a high relevance. If their heading is only slightly different, static movement will cause them to never reach the vicinity of the receiver, leading to a low relevance. The large difference in relevance is not plausible since vehicles can easily change their headings, especially if they are not too fast and still far away. This will be accounted by the relevance function that will be presented in this paper.

2.5   Situation Assessment

In the last years vehicular systems for environment perception made a huge step in microscopic situation assessment. Based on radar and cameras, sophisticated algorithms assess the situation and evaluate different movement paths [13][14]. Work from this area has two drawbacks which prohibit their usage in our context: Its microscopic perspective is related to the direct vicinity of vehicles, while we want to cover an area of about 1000 m radius. Also situation assessment algorithms require powerful processing units and base on complex physical and mathematic models for only few vehicles in parallel.

3   Derivation of an Improved Relevance Estimation Function

In this section we derive an improved relevance estimation function by extending the simple relevance estimation function from Equation (1). We use a receiver-centric notation to keep the equations simple. The circular path movement approach allows for changes in the heading of vehicles over time. Accelerations allow for speed changes over time. Additional improvements aim at a more sophisticated distance determination formula replacing $d(\alpha, \beta, t)$ while keeping the rest of the relevance estimation formula $R(\alpha, \beta)$ the same as described in Equation (1). In the last section we discuss shortcomings of our proposals.

3.1   Receiver-Centric Notation

In the following we use a receiver-centric translation of original positions and movement vectors of both sender and receiver [8]. This allows us to use some simplifications in the following sections which do not change basic ideas and results but facilitate an easier notation. The receiver is still and located in the origin of a two-dimensional coordinate system. The sender is located relatively to the receiver such that its relative movement vector is pointing horizontally from right to left.

We denote the translated position of a sender by $\mathbf{p}_\alpha^{\text{rel}} = \begin{pmatrix} x_\alpha^{\text{rel}} \\ y_\alpha^{\text{rel}} \end{pmatrix}$ and the movement vector by $\mathbf{v}_\alpha^{\text{rel}} = \begin{pmatrix} v_\alpha^{\text{rel}} \\ 0 \end{pmatrix}$. The receivers position and movement vectors correspond to the null vector in receiver-centric notation.

3.2 Circular Path Movement

This section describes how sender movement on a circular path can be added to the simple relevance estimation function. First, we explain the basic idea, then we show how physical effects leading to a minimum curve radius can be respected.

Basic Idea. The basic idea behind a circular path movement extrapolation is the pessimistic assumption that the sender will head towards the receiver's position and eventually collide.

To collide with the receiver, we allow a continuous change of direction that results in a circular movement of the sender. The receiver "attracts" the sender like a magnet, i.e., the sender changes its heading continuously over time. Figure 1 depicts this approach. Sender α_{right} is located to the right of the receiver and sender α_{left} is located to the left of the receiver. Both are initially driving horizontally from right to left. According to the circular movement model they change their heading in a way that they eventually reach the receiver's position. If vehicles keep their speed and change only their headings, they will follow the arcs $b_{\text{forward}}^{\text{left}}$ or $b_{\text{forward}}^{\text{right}}$, respectively. However, they may easily change their relative movement by braking or accelerating backwards so that they also could approach the receiver on the arcs $b_{\text{backward}}^{\text{left}}$ or $b_{\text{backward}}^{\text{right}}$, respectively. In the following, we derive formulae for senders to the right of the receiver ($x_\alpha > 0$ m). Similar formulae exist for senders to the left of the receiver.

The positions of both sender and receiver and the initial heading of the sender define a circle. Its center has the coordinates

$$\mathbf{P}_c = \begin{pmatrix} x_\alpha^{\text{rel}} \\ -\frac{1}{2} \cdot \frac{(x_\alpha^{\text{rel}})^2 - (y_\alpha^{\text{rel}})^2}{y_\alpha^{\text{rel}}} \end{pmatrix}. \tag{3}$$

The radius r of the circle is given by

$$r = \frac{1}{2} \cdot \frac{(x_\alpha^{\text{rel}})^2 - (y_\alpha^{\text{rel}})^2}{y_\alpha^{\text{rel}}}. \tag{4}$$

The length of the arc $b_{\text{forward}}^{\text{right}}$ can by calculated by

$$b_{\text{forward}}^{\text{right}} = 2 \cdot r \cdot \arcsin\left(\frac{|\mathbf{P}_\alpha^{\text{rel}}|}{2 \cdot r}\right). \tag{5}$$

The length of arc $b_{\text{backward}}^{\text{right}}$ can be derived accordingly. If we allow sender vehicles to change heading, we implicitly assume that they move on a circular arc. As

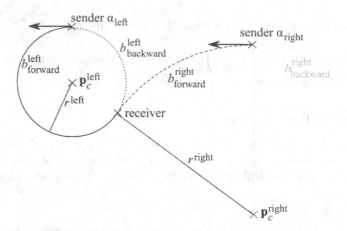

Fig. 1. Circular movement of sending vehicles towards the receiving vehicle; the illustrated movement is relative to the receiver's position

a consequence, we need to respect that in the distance calculation required for Equation (1). The adapted distance function is

$$d_{\text{arc}}^{\text{circular}}(\alpha, \beta, t) = b_{\text{forward}}^{\text{right}} - |\mathbf{v}_\alpha^{\text{rel}}| \cdot t, \tag{6}$$

which replaces $d(\alpha, \beta, t)$ in Equation (1).

In [8] we derived an analytical expression for the maximum value of Equation (1) so that it could be easily calculated. This expression can be adapted to the modified distance function $d_{\text{arc}}^{\text{circular}}(\alpha, \beta, t)$.

Minimum Curve Radius. In the preceding section we described how a circular path movement can be realized. This model gives reasonable results, but is inaccurate by allowing very small curve radii. Considering the centrifugal force, the curve radius at a specific speed v cannot be lower than

$$r_{\min}(v) = \frac{v^2}{g \cdot \mu}, \tag{7}$$

where g corresponds to the force of gravity and μ is the friction value [15].

If the speed for a given sending vehicle is too high, it might be physically impossible for it to collide with the receiver because that would require a too small curve radius. As a consequence, the circular path derived in Section 3.2 is not valid. Therefore, we assume that the vehicle follows a circular path with the minimum radius $r_{\min}$ as computed in Equation (7). Since the proposed arc does not link sender and receiver, we use the straight-line distance as distance measure under these conditions:

$$
d_{\text{straight}}^{\text{circular}}(\alpha, \beta, r, t, \mathbf{v}_\alpha^{\text{rel}}) =
$$

$$
\left\| \begin{pmatrix} x_\alpha - \sin\left(\frac{|\mathbf{v}_\alpha^{\text{rel}}|}{\max(r, r_{\min}(|\mathbf{v}_\alpha|))}t\right) \cdot \max(r, r_{\min}(|\mathbf{v}_\alpha|)) \\ y_\alpha - \cos\left(\frac{|\mathbf{v}_\alpha^{\text{rel}}|}{\max(r, r_{\min}(|\mathbf{v}_\alpha|))}t\right) \cdot \max(r, r_{\min}(|\mathbf{v}_\alpha|)) \end{pmatrix} \right\| \tag{8}
$$

To keep things simple and avoid discontinuities we also use the straight-line distance for senders and receivers that may collide.

3.3 Accelerations

One drawback of the simple relevance estimation function is the assumption of constant speed, because each vehicle might slow down or speed up after the message is sent.

Changes in speed may have the effect that a short distance on the arc in Equation (6) or a short straight-line distance in Equation (8) may be reached earlier than without acceleration which increases the maximum relevance value of a message.

In this section we consider positive and negative accelerations of the sender in the relevance function. First, we introduce a function which utilizes constant accelerations, then we allow for speed-dependent acceleration.

Constant Acceleration. We first propose to integrate a "worst-case" acceleration $a_{\max}$ in the distance function. The value for $a_{\max}$ can be taken from empirical studies [16].

Constant accelerations can be integrated into Equation (8) by replacing $|\mathbf{v}_\alpha^{\text{rel}}|$ with the term $|\mathbf{v}_\alpha^{\text{rel}}| \cdot t + \frac{1}{2} \cdot a_{\max} \cdot t^2$. As $r_{\min}(v)$ depends on the speed, we take the maximum sender speed $v_{\max}$ between t_{now} and $t_{\text{now}} + T_{\max}$ as input. These changes yield

$$
d_{\text{straight}}^{\text{const. acc.}}(\alpha, \beta, r, t, \mathbf{v}_\alpha^{\text{rel}}) =
$$

$$
\left\| \begin{pmatrix} x_\alpha - \sin\left(\frac{|\mathbf{v}_\alpha^{\text{rel}}| \cdot t + \frac{1}{2} \cdot a_{\max} \cdot t^2}{\max(r, r_{\min}(v_{\max}))}t\right) \cdot \max(r, r_{\min}(v_{\max})) \\ y_\alpha - \cos\left(\frac{|\mathbf{v}_\alpha^{\text{rel}}| \cdot t + \frac{1}{2} \cdot a_{\max} \cdot t^2}{\max(r, r_{\min}(v_{\max}))}t\right) \cdot \max(r, r_{\min}(v_{\max})) \end{pmatrix} \right\| \tag{9}
$$

Speed-Dependent Acceleration. The assumption of constant acceleration is not considering the vehicles' current speeds and leads to unrealistic speed changes. In reality, the maximum achievable acceleration depends on the current speed.

We now introduce an algorithm for relevance estimation based on speed-dependent acceleration. The algorithm has three steps. First, we determine the maximum speed of the sending vehicle. Second, we check if this maximum speed is too high for the curve radius needed to collide with the receiver. Third, we iterate over all time steps in the respective time interval to extrapolate the movement and calculate the relevance value for each time step. The maximum relevance value of this iteration yields the overall relevance value. The following sections refer to Algorithm 1.

Algorithm 1. Calculation of the relevance value R

Input   : Curve radius r, absolute sender speed $|\mathbf{v}_\alpha|$, starting time t_{now},
                extrapolation time $T_{\max}$, time step duration Δt, minimum distance
                $d_{\min}$, time penalty exponent γ, sender α, and receiver β

```
// Step 1: Determine the maximum speed v_max
```
1   $v \leftarrow |\mathbf{v}_\alpha|$;   `// Initial speed`
2   $t \leftarrow t_{\text{now}}$;
3   **repeat**
4 | $a \leftarrow a(v)$;   `// Target accelerations from Table 1`
5 | $v \leftarrow v + \Delta t \cdot a$;   `// Calculate new speed`
6 | $t \leftarrow t + \Delta t$;
7   **until** $t > t_{\text{now}} + T_{\max}$;
8   $v_{\max} \leftarrow v$;
```
// Step 2: Check if curve radius r is less than r_min(v_max)
```
9   **if** $r < r_{\min}(v_{\max})$ **then**
10 | $r \leftarrow r_{\min}(v_{\max})$;   `// Use minimum curve radius`
11 **end**
```
// Step 3: Calculate the relevance value R iteratively
```
12 $R \leftarrow -\infty$;
13 $t \leftarrow t_{\text{now}}$;
14 **repeat**
15 | $d \leftarrow d^{\text{circular}}_{\text{straight}}(\alpha, \beta, r, t, v)$;   `// Calculate sender and receiver distance`
16 | $R \leftarrow \max\left(R, \frac{\text{m}}{\max(d, d_{\min})} \cdot \frac{1}{(1 + \frac{t}{8})^\gamma}\right)$;   `// Maximum relevance until t`
17 | $t \leftarrow t + \Delta t$;
18 **until** $t > t_{\text{now}} + T_{\max}$;
Output: Relevance value R

Step 1: Determination of the Maximum Speed of the Sender (Lines 1–8). We first determine the maximum sender speed $v_{\max}$ in the interval from t_{now} to $t_{\text{now}} + T_{\max}$ in steps with duration Δt.

Initially, speed variable v is set to the sender's absolute speed $|\mathbf{v}_\alpha|$. For each time step we extract the current acceleration a with function $a(v)$ from a lookup table for the current speed v. Eventually, this yields the maximum speed $v_{\max}$ in the considered time interval. The minimum (negative) speed can be derived accordingly.

We use lookup tables to assign accelerations to speeds. Table 1 and Table 2 provide the values we used for positive and negative accelerations, respectively. The values can be extracted from empirical studies [16]. The accelerations decrease with higher speeds. Decelerations are high for positive speeds to allow for full braking, while driving backwards enables only low decelerations.

Step 2: Minimum Curve Radius Check (Lines 9–11). We use the maximum speed $v_{\max}$ in Equation (7) to determine whether the calculated curve radius r from Equation (4) for a collision of sender and receiver is too small. If that is the case, $r_{\min}$ replaces r as curve radius in the following calculations.

In our proposal we do not consider changing minimal curve radii due to changing speeds over time. Such an approach would lead to multiple possible paths

Table 1. Used acceleration values (* taken from [16])

Speed	Acceleration
$0 < v \le 60 \ \frac{km}{h}$	$3.79 \ \frac{m}{s^2}$ *
$60 \ \frac{km}{h} < v \le 80 \ \frac{km}{h}$	$3.42 \ \frac{m}{s^2}$ *
$80 \ \frac{km}{h} < v \le 100 \ \frac{km}{h}$	$2.83 \ \frac{m}{s^2}$ *
$100 \ \frac{km}{h} < v \le 120 \ \frac{km}{h}$	$2.43 \ \frac{m}{s^2}$ *
$120 \ \frac{km}{h} < v$	$1.5 \ \frac{m}{s^2}$

Table 2. Used deceleration values (* taken from [16])

Speed	Deceleration
$0 < v$	$10.5 \ \frac{m}{s^2}$ *
$-10 \ \frac{km}{h} < v \le 0 \ \frac{km}{h}$	$1 \ \frac{m}{s^2}$
$v \le -10 \ \frac{km}{h}$	$0 \ \frac{km}{h}$

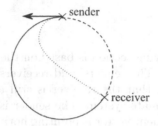

Fig. 2. The circular path might not be the fastest way for the sender to reach the receiver

the vehicles could take in order to collide. This is an optimization problem which would be too inefficient to solve for our operational scenario.

Step 3: Maximizing the Relevance Value (Lines 12–18). We calculate the relevance value in an iterative way. For each time step we first calculate the distance between sender and receiver d. We use this distance to calculate the relevance value for each time step. The resulting maximum relevance value R is an approximation for the result of Equation (1) with distance function $d_{\text{straight}}^{\text{circular}}(\alpha, \beta, r, t, v)$.

3.4 Criticism

The presented approach may not find the fastest path for the sender to reach the receiver and, therefore, yield too low relevance values. Figure 2 illustrates an example: our approach supports movement on the solid and dashed line paths. Instead, the sender may drive on the dotted path by first taking a turn with low speed and accelerate afterwards. Depending on the initial conditions, this path may lead to higher relevance values.

When a vehicle accelerates, it may first drive a narrow curve at low speed and a wider curve only at high speed. In sum, the vehicle may have changed its direction more than under the assumption that the minimum radius of the curve was governed by the maximum speed. Thereby, the relevance of senders in some positions may be underestimated.

A shortcoming of the proposed functions is that they do not yet account for potential movement changes of the receiver. That is also relevant: a sender may follow a receiver both driving at 200 $\frac{km}{h}$. While the sender can hardly accelerate at that speed, the receiver can brake which quickly reduces the distance between the two vehicles.

4   Evaluation

In this section we evaluate the improved relevance estimation function. First, we describe the evaluation methodology. Then, we demonstrate the impact of different parameter sets on the relevance values.

4.1   Methodology

The evaluation in the following section is based on the receiver-centric notation as described in Section 3.1. The senders' and receivers' position and movement vectors are translated such that the receiver is still and located in the origin of a two-dimensional coordinate system. The sender is located relatively to the receiver such that its movement vector is pointing horizontally from right to left.

If not stated differently, we set $d_{min} = 10$ m and $T_{max} = 8$ s. We set the time penalty exponent such that $(1 + \frac{T_{max}}{s})^{-\gamma} = 0.3$, i.e., $\gamma = -\frac{\ln(0.3)}{\ln(1 + \frac{T_{max}}{s})} = 0.548$ to prevent steep transitions for distant senders.

We evaluate the relevance estimation function by calculating the relevance values for all sender positions in a 160 m × 300 m rectangle around a potential receiver. The selectable parameters for the experiment are d_{min}, T_{max}, γ, $|v_\alpha^{rel}|$, and $|v_\alpha|$. Figures 3(a)–3(f) show the results of our experiments. The x- and y-axis indicate the position of a sender relative to the receiver. The color in the figures indicates the relevance of the sender due to its position and other parameters. The diagrams below the figures show the relevance of senders with $y = 0$ m depending on their x-positions. In the following, we discuss these diagrams for different sets of selectable parameters.

4.2   Impact of Relative Speed $|v_\alpha^{rel}|$ and Sender Speed $|v_\alpha|$

In Figure 3(a) the initial relative speed of sender and receiver is $0 \frac{m}{s}$ and the absolute speed of the sender $|v_\alpha|$ is also $0 \frac{m}{s}$, i.e., both vehicles are standing still. We identify two effects. First, the area from where senders are able to reach the vicinity of the receiver within time T_{max} is curved. This is caused by the consideration of a circular path movement as described in Section 3.2. Second, the areas above and below the center of the upper plot have a significantly lower relevance value. This effect is caused by the minimum curve radius implementation. Senders originating in these areas cannot reach the vicinity of the receiver on a circular path at their current speed and, therefore, their relevance is low.

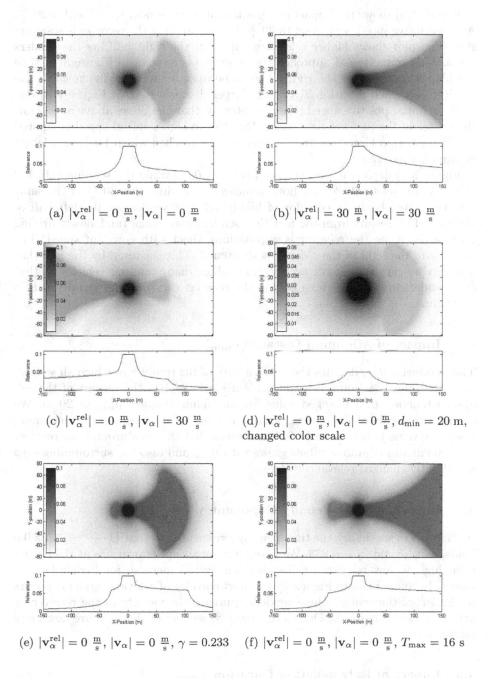

(a) $|\mathbf{v}_\alpha^{\mathrm{rel}}| = 0 \ \frac{\mathrm{m}}{\mathrm{s}}, \ |\mathbf{v}_\alpha| = 0 \ \frac{\mathrm{m}}{\mathrm{s}}$

(b) $|\mathbf{v}_\alpha^{\mathrm{rel}}| = 30 \ \frac{\mathrm{m}}{\mathrm{s}}, \ |\mathbf{v}_\alpha| = 30 \ \frac{\mathrm{m}}{\mathrm{s}}$

(c) $|\mathbf{v}_\alpha^{\mathrm{rel}}| = 0 \ \frac{\mathrm{m}}{\mathrm{s}}, \ |\mathbf{v}_\alpha| = 30 \ \frac{\mathrm{m}}{\mathrm{s}}$

(d) $|\mathbf{v}_\alpha^{\mathrm{rel}}| = 0 \ \frac{\mathrm{m}}{\mathrm{s}}, \ |\mathbf{v}_\alpha| = 0 \ \frac{\mathrm{m}}{\mathrm{s}}, \ d_{\mathrm{min}} = 20 \ \mathrm{m}$, changed color scale

(e) $|\mathbf{v}_\alpha^{\mathrm{rel}}| = 0 \ \frac{\mathrm{m}}{\mathrm{s}}, \ |\mathbf{v}_\alpha| = 0 \ \frac{\mathrm{m}}{\mathrm{s}}, \ \gamma = 0.233$

(f) $|\mathbf{v}_\alpha^{\mathrm{rel}}| = 0 \ \frac{\mathrm{m}}{\mathrm{s}}, \ |\mathbf{v}_\alpha| = 0 \ \frac{\mathrm{m}}{\mathrm{s}}, \ T_{\mathrm{max}} = 16 \ \mathrm{s}$

Fig. 3. Relevance values for senders moving from right to left depending on position and speed relative to a sender at the origin. The upper parts of the figures show the spatial results, whereas the lower parts are a cross-section for y-position 0 m (default values $\gamma = 0.548$, $T_{\mathrm{max}} = 8 \ \mathrm{s}$, and $d_{\mathrm{min}} = 10 \ \mathrm{m}$).

Figure 3(b) shows the impact of a positive absolute sender speed $|\mathbf{v}_\alpha| = 30 \frac{m}{s}$. As the relative speed $|\mathbf{v}_\alpha^{rel}|$ is set to $30 \frac{m}{s}$, this means that the receiver is standing still. The plot shows higher relevance values in the right half, as the senders are moving initially and approach the receiver faster than in Figure 3(a). The corridor is extended to the right. This is because senders driving towards the receiver can reach it within T_{max} from larger distance than in Figure 3(a) due to their initial positive speed. We also observe that the areas above and below the center of the plot are now wider. Due to the higher initial speed compared to Figure 3(a), a larger maximum speed can be reached which leads to a larger minimum curve radius.

Figure 3(c) depicts a relative speed $|\mathbf{v}_\alpha^{rel}|$ of $0 \frac{m}{s}$, while the sending vehicles' speed $|\mathbf{v}_\alpha|$ is set to $30 \frac{m}{s}$, i.e., both vehicles are driving with $30 \frac{m}{s}$ in the same direction. We observe a corridor of highly relevant senders in the left half of the plot. This results from the fact that senders may brake (and slowly driving backwards) while the receiver is approaching them with constant speed. The corridor to the right of the receiver is shortened. This is caused by the fact that fast driving cars have lower acceleration values than standing vehicles so that only senders in a smaller area behind the receiver can reach its vicinity within short time.

4.3   Impact of Minimum Distance d_{min}

The parameter d_{min} denotes the near vicinity of the receiver in which all senders have the same maximum relevance. Figure 3(d) depicts the output of the relevance function of a changed value for minimum distance d_{min} of 20 m. We changed the scale of the coloring in this particular plot because the maximum relevance value is now $\frac{1}{20} = 0.05$. We observe that the area around the receiver with maximum relevance values grows with d_{min} and also the surrounding area has slightly changed relevance values.

4.4   Impact of Time Penalty Exponent γ

In Figure 3(e) we change the time penalty exponent such that $(1 + \frac{T_{max}}{s})^{-\gamma} = 0.6$ holds, which yields $\gamma = 0.233$. We observe more abrupt transitions at the border from high to low relevance values and an overall increase for high relevance values. In comparison to Figure 3(a) a short corridor of relevant senders appears to the left of the center. These senders approach the vicinity of the receiver by driving slowly backwards. Due to the lower γ, senders in this area are now more relevant.

4.5   Impact of Extrapolation Duration T_{max}

In Figure 3(f) the extrapolation duration T_{max} is set to 16 s, i.e., the time interval for movement extrapolation T_{max} is doubled. Compared to Figure 3(a), the corridor of high relevance grows to the right, and we observe a bigger area of low relevance above and below the center of the plot; the latter is due to a larger minimum curve radius which needs to be respected if T_{max} is longer because then a higher extrapolated speed can be reached. A short corridor of senders to the left of the receiver also gains enough negative speed to approach the receiver, which leads to high relevance values for these senders.

5   Conclusion and Future Work

Each vehicle equipped with VANET technology will receive Cooperative Awareness Messages (CAMs) from neighboring vehicles and infrastructure. Series vehicles have to be able to process high rates of CAMs if the technology's penetration rate rises and local traffic is dense. In an earlier work we proposed a relevance estimation function which determines a relevance value for each received CAM based on basic information like position and movement without a map. This approach utilized static movement extrapolation which may not be realistic enough to estimate good relevance values. In this paper, we proposed a more sophisticated relevance estimation function that considers changes in heading and speed of the sending vehicles.

Before the improved relevance estimation function can be integrated into a series system, one has to evaluate the functions' results for real or simulated traffic and its ability to predict relevance via extrapolation. We may have to augment the improved function with further effects such as potential movement changes of the receiver which are not yet considered in this work. The used parameters have to be tuned to conform to typical vehicular behavior. To facilitate an efficient implementation, we propose to determine relevance values in a vehicular implementation by using a characteristic diagram.

References

1. Sichitiu, M., Kihl, M.: Inter-Vehicle Communication Systems: A Survey. IEEE Communications Surveys & Tutorials 10(2), 88–105 (2008)
2. CAR 2 CAR Communication Consortium: Memorandum of Understanding for OEMs within the CAR 2 CAR Communication Consortium on Deployment Strategy for Cooperative ITS in Europe (2011)
3. Weiß, C.: V2X Communication in Europe – From Research Projects Towards Standardization and Field Testing of Vehicle Communication Technology. Computer Networks 55(14), 3103–3119 (2011)
4. European Telecommunications Standards Institute (ETSI): Intelligent Transport Systems (ITS); Vehicular Communications; Basic Set of Applications; Part 3: Specifications of Decentralized Environmental Notification Basic Service (102 637-3) (2010)
5. European Telecommunications Standards Institute (ETSI): Intelligent Transport Systems (ITS); Vehicular Communications; Basic Set of Applications; Part 2: Specification of Cooperative Awareness Basic Service (302 637-2) (2011)
6. ABI Research: V2V Penetration in New Vehicles to Reach 62% by 2027 (2013)
7. Kraftfahrt-Bundesamt: Fahrzeugzulassungen (FZ); Bestand an Kraftfahrzeugen und Kraftfahrzeuganhängern nach Fahrzeugalter (January 1, 2012)

8. Breu, J., Menth, M.: Relevance Estimation of Cooperative Awareness Messages in VANETs. In: Proceedings of the 5th International Symposium on Wireless Vehicular Communications (2013)
9. Stubing, H., Bechler, M., Heussner, D., May, T., Radusch, I., Rechner, H., Vogel, P.: simTD: A Car-to-X System Architecture for Field Operational Tests. IEEE Communications Magazine 48(5), 148–154 (2010)
10. Wilbrod, J.H., Segarra, G.: Systéme Coopératif Routier Expérimental @ France (2012)
11. Festag, A., Le, L., Goleva, M.: Field Operational Tests for Cooperative Systems: a Tussle Between Research, Standardization and Deployment. In: Proceedings of the 8th ACM International Workshop on Vehicular Inter-Networking, pp. 73–78. ACM, New York (2011)
12. Breu, J., Brakemeier, A., Menth, M.: Relevance Estimation of Cooperative Awareness Messages in VANETs. In: Proceedings of the 13th International Conference on ITS Telecommunications (ITST), pp. 8–13 (2013)
13. Tamke, A., Dang, T., Breuel, G.: A Flexible Method for Criticality Assessment in Driver Assistance Systems. In: Proceedings of the 2011 Intelligent Vehicles Symposium (2011)
14. Hillenbrand, J., Kroschel, K., Schmid, V.: Situation assessment algorithm for a collision prevention assistant. In: Proceedings of the 2005 Intelligent Vehicles Symposium (2005)
15. Blau, P.J.: Friction Science and Technology. CRC Press (1995)
16. Burg, H., Moser, A.: Handbuch Verkehrsunfallrekonstruktion. Vieweg+Teubner (2009)

Evaluation of Performance Enhancement
for Crash Constellation Prediction
via Car-to-Car Communication
A Simulation Model Based Approach

Thomas Kuehbeck[1], Gor Hakobyan[1], Axel Sikora[2], Claude C. Chibelushi[3],
and Mansour Moniri[3]

[1] BMW AG, Germany
[2] HS Offenburg, Germany
[3] Staffordshire University, UK

Abstract. Active safety systems for advanced driver assistance systems
act within a complex, dynamic traffic environment featuring various
sensor systems which detect the vehicles' surroundings and interior. This
paper describes the recent progress towards a performance evaluation of
car-to-car communication (C2C) for active safety systems - in particular
for crash constellation prediction. The methodology introduced in this work
is designed to evaluate the impact of different sensors on the accuracy of
a crash constellation prediction algorithm. The benefit of C2C communication (viewed as a virtual sensor) within a sensor data fusion architecture for pre-crash collision prediction is explored. Therefore, a simulation
environment for accident scenarios analysis reproducing real-world sensor
behaviour, is designed and implemented. Performance evaluation results
show that C2C increases confidence in the estimated position of the oncoming vehicle. With C2C enhancement the given accuracy in time-to-collision
(TTC) estimation is achievable about 110 ms earlier for moderate velocities at TTC range of [0.5s..0.2s]. The uncertainty in the vehicle position
prediction at the time of collision can be reduced about half by integrating
C2C communication into the sensor data fusion.

1 Introduction

Today's safety technology in motor vehicles requires sophisticated information
about an impending collision, to prepare and trigger active safety systems (e.g.
collision warning, brake assist, traction control, etc.) and passive safety systems
(e.g. belt systems, airbags, etc.) to mitigate the severity of the accident for all
involved parties. To meet these requirements, a fusion of sensors such as lidar,
radar, and vision-based systems is needed for measuring the relative movements
of the other vehicle involved in the accident and detecting a collision when it is
inevitable. The severity of the collision directly depends on parameters describing
the constellation of the crash. The parameters affecting the severity of a vehicle-
to-vehicle collision are identified in various publications [2, 14, 9, 16].

A. Sikora et al. (Eds.): Nets4Cars/Nets4Trains/Nets4Aircraft 2014, LNCS 8435, pp. 57–68, 2014.

Knowing the constellation of an impending collision, such as at the point-of-no-return, when no physical trajectories allow crash avoidance, enables the use of active safety counter measures to mitigate the collision. Safety systems, such as active seats, restraint-systems, or airbags, can be activated to an extent adapted to the crash constellation. To guarantee fault-free triggering of such systems, the sensors need to detect the dynamic characteristics of the impending collision at a very high accuracy.

In the presented work C2C communication is modelled as an enhancement for crash constellation prediction system to evaluate the prediction accuracy improvement resulting from C2C. The enhancement of the sensor data fusion via C2C provides extended information about the velocity, acceleration, and steerage of the target vehicle to the state estimation and trajectory planning modules, allowing improved prediction of the path of the target vehicle. The present approach to evaluate the performance enhancement includes an identification of the parameters influencing crash severity; a simulation framework simulating the real world behaviour of a state-of-the-art sensor fusion system including state estimation and object tracking; and a constellation extraction algorithm.

The rest of the paper is organised as follows: Section 2 provides an overview of crash constellation parameter's identification and constellation extraction. The simulation framework, including the system model, state estimation, C2C communication and crash constellation prediction are described in Section 3. The simulation results are provided in Section 4, followed by the description of the model validation. Section 5 concludes presented performance analysis.

2   The Concept of Crash Constellation Prediction

2.1   Identification of Parameters Which Significantly Influence the Severity of a Crash

Analyses on accident databases, such as the German In-Depth Accident Study (GIDAS) database [6], are essential for identifying the key parameters defining the severity of a crash [2, 6, 9, 14, 16]. An overview of the latest analyses on accident databases according to the method used is given in [14].

The independent variables contain different characteristics: road and environment, human, vehicle, and crash. For the dependent variables constituting the output, different scales are used, impeding an objective interpretation. Therefore, the approaches applying the Abbreviated Injury Scale (AIS) or Injury Severity Score (ISS) as dependent variables are considered here for the identification of the crash parameters allowing an objective comparison. Furthermore, evaluation of advanced safety systems such as ABS, ESP, or airbags requires restricting to new vehicles [13].

Crash constellation parameters are described in detail in [3, 5, 10, 15]. From the complete set of parameters, the following can be reconstructed from sensory data and are considered here:

1. Relative velocity.
2. Impact angle between the vehicles.
3. Collision point.
4. Alignment offset (overlap).
5. Estimated TTC (Time-to-collision).

These major parameters are used in the simulation model to evaluate the accuracy of the constellation extraction.

2.2   Crash Prediction and Constellation Extraction

Crash prediction and constellation extraction are affected directly by the quality of the underlying trajectory forecasting algorithm. The accuracy of trajectory calculation itself depends on the precision of state estimation. Trajectories help to predict the motion of the ego-vehicle and the motion of other entities within the neighbourhood of the vehicle. This information about the surrounding environment allows the detection of hazardous situations [8, 11]. In particular, a crash is unavoidable for a given vehicle, if all calculated trajectories end in an obstacle. If a crash is likely to occur, the point of no return is defined as the point at which no action can prevent an accident.

The crash parameters are designed according to the GIDAS specification defining the collision point with two parameters incorporating the distance of the collision point to the front centre of the vehicle. In the current implementation the collision point is defined as the first point of impact, thus, it is on the edge of the symbolic rectangle representing the vehicle. As these parameters are dependent, one of the collision parameters is replaced with the rectangle edge which contains the collision point.

The collision point is now defined by (i.e. vehicle near-side, off-side, front, or back) and the distance from the point to the front centre of the vehicle along that colliding edge. Figure 1 gives a graphical representation of the collision point metric.

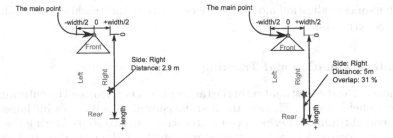

Fig. 1. Top-view depiction of a crash between the ego-vehicle (with labelled front, rear, left, and right sides) and an obstacle, which could be another vehicle. The collision point is shown by the star in the left picture, and the collision overlap is the relative length of the line which joins the two stars in the right picture.

As shown in Figure 1, the overlap of a collision is calculated as the relative length of the orthogonal projection of the colliding edge of the obstacle (e.g. another vehicle, for example) onto the colliding edge of the ego-vehicle. This overlap is measured as a percentage relative to the length of the colliding side of the ego-vehicle.

3   Simulation Framework and Modules

The crash constellation prediction accuracy enhancement analysis limits the possibilities of real-world evaluation, as it is performed during the pre-crash phase. This paved the way for a simulation framework enabling arbitrary collision scenario definition between two vehicles featuring a real world sensor behaviour enhanced with C2C communication. Furthermore, algorithms for state estimation based crash constellation extraction have been applied. All these components allow a performance analysis by comparing the crash parameter prediction precision in different collision scenarios regarding the C2C enhancement. The following section describes the system model of the simulation framework including its main components.

3.1   System Model

For simplicity, the simulation is performed in 2D space, thus, the z coordinate, and the roll and pitch angles are not considered. The state of the ego vehicle is considered to be perfectly known. For vehicle dynamics a single-track model is utilised. Once any point of the target vehicle enters the field of view of the ego vehicle, state estimation based on the extended Kalman filter (EKF) is performed. The crash constellation is predicted iteratively based on the ground truth of the time-to-collision calculation and starts at a certain time (500 ms, in the work reported in this paper) before the collision. The ground truth of the collision parameters serves as a reference for further comparison to predicted parameters.

The entire framework includes the following modules: graphical user interface, vehicle dynamics realisation module, state estimation and tracking, and collision parameters extraction.

3.2   State Estimation and Tracking

As mentioned, the state estimation of the target object is performed by entering the ego vehicle's field of view. Thereby the first measurement is used for initialisation of the extended Kalman filter performing iteratively in two steps. During the first step, the state vector $\hat{x}$ (Eq. 1) of the target vehicle at the next time instance is calculated, together with the prediction uncertainty matrix P (Eq. 2).

$$\hat{x}_{k|k-1} = f(\hat{x}_{k|k-1}, u_{k-1}) \tag{1}$$

$$P_{k|k-1} = F_{k-1}P_{(k-1|k-1)}F_{k-1}^T + Q_{k-1} \tag{2}$$

where u_{k-1} is the control input, Q_{k-1} is the process noise covariance matrix, and F_{k-1} is the Jacobian of the function $f((\hat{x}_{k|k-1}, u_{k-1}))$ defined in Eq. 3. Analogously, H_k is the Jacobian of the function $h(x_{k|\hat{k}-1})$, which maps the true state space into measurement space.

$$F_{k-1} = J_k^F = \frac{\partial}{\partial x}f(x)\Big|_{x=\hat{x}_{k-1|k-1}} \qquad H_k = J_k^H = \frac{\partial}{\partial x}h(x)\Big|_{x=\hat{x}_{k-1|k-1}} \tag{3}$$

Once the measurement is available, the Kalman gain is calculated according to Eq. 4.

$$K(t_k) = P_{k|k-1}H_k^T(H_k P_{k|k-1}H_k^T + R_k) \tag{4}$$

where R_k is the measurement noise covariance matrix. Afterwards, the predicted state vector as well as the uncertainty covariance are updated by the Kalman gain as shown in Eq. 5 and 6.

$$\hat{x}_{k|k} = \hat{x}_{k|k-1} + K_k(z_k - h(\hat{x}_{k|k-1})) \tag{5}$$
$$P_{k|k} = [I - K_k H_k]P_{k|k-1} \tag{6}$$

where z_k is the measurement, and I is the identity matrix.

Since, in reality the target vehicle's state estimation is performed in the ego vehicle's coordinate system, coordinate transformations as well as ego motion compensation are required. The ego-motion compensated and predicted state for time instance k in case of an additional acceleration vector estimation is calculated using the predicted state $\hat{x}_{t_{k|k-1}}$

$$\hat{x}_{k|k-1} = f_{ego}[\hat{x}_{t_{k|k-1}}, \hat{u}_{ego_k}] = \begin{bmatrix} R_{ego}^T \cdot \left(\begin{bmatrix} x_t \\ y_t \end{bmatrix} - \begin{bmatrix} \Delta x_{ego} \\ \Delta y_{ego} \end{bmatrix} \right) \\ R_{ego}^T \cdot \begin{bmatrix} v_{x_t} \\ v_{y_t} \end{bmatrix} \\ R_{ego}^T \cdot \begin{bmatrix} a_{x_t} \\ a_{y_t} \end{bmatrix} \end{bmatrix} \tag{7}$$

R_{ego}^T is the transpose of the rotation matrix defined as

$$R_{ego} = \begin{bmatrix} \cos\psi & -\sin\psi \\ \sin\psi & \cos\psi \end{bmatrix} \tag{8}$$

where ψ is the yaw rate of the ego vehicle. Δx_{ego} and Δy_{ego} describe the coordinate change of the host vehicle.

Sensor data fusion performance is selected accordingly to the covariance matrix measured in the real test vehicle. Assuming time invariant measurement and process noise, the covariance matrix at the output of the extended Kalman filter converges against a certain value. Hence, a relationship between measurement matrix R and covariance matrix $P = P_t = P_{t-1}$ can be derived:

$$R = \left(\left(I - \frac{P}{P_{k|k-1}} \right) / H \right) \backslash (P_{k|k-1}H^T) - HP_{k|k-1}H^T \tag{9}$$

where $P_{k|k-1}$ is

$$P_{k|k-1} = F_k P F_k^T + Q_k \tag{10}$$

where F is the motion model and Q is the process noise matrix. A white noise acceleration model is utilised as a second order kinematic motion model ($\sigma_{a_x} = \sigma_{a_y} = 4 \; m/s^2$ [7]).

Though, the measurement noise covariance in reality might be time variable depending on many circumstances, Eq. 9 is a good approximation to reproduce the performance of the real sensor fusion in the simulation model. So, specifying the covariance matrix of the sensor data fusion from real world data allows the approximation of the sensor fusion performance within the model.

3.3   C2C Communication

Since C2C communication delivers additional information about the environment and about the target vehicle particularly, it can be seen as a virtual sensor. The information delivered via C2C communication is directly measured by in-vehicle sensors of the target vehicle, thus, is much more precise than the target's state measurements received through ego-vehicle sensors [11]. The latency, accompanying the information exchange, is constant, which enables accurate compensation, resulting in a high precision in calculation of the object's state [11]. Hence, in the simulation framework C2C communication is modelled to deliver more precise velocity measurements (σ_v =0.1 m/s), as well as high precision acceleration measurements (σ_a =0.1 m/s^2).

Furthermore, some additional information can be provided by the target vehicle (acceleration, driver's current intention, etc.), which can hardly be captured via ego-vehicle sensors. This information complements the ego-vehicle's awareness of the environment and can be used to enhance the functionality of different ADAS. In the simulation framework, the information about the driver's immediate intention is accounted for in the calculation of possible trajectories.

3.4   Crash Constellation Prediction

The prediction of collision parameters is based on the state estimation of the target vehicle. First, an estimated state vector of the target vehicle is used to calculate possible trajectories the target vehicle could take. Depending on the magnitude and direction of the acceleration vector various trajectories are possible. As it is known, these trajectories are limited by physical constraints. Thereby also the maximum possible acceleration of the vehicle is limited. The trajectory bounds (referred to herein as maximum trajectories) are the ones achievable with an acceleration vector pointing in different directions (Kamm's circle [12]). This constraint is used for calculating possible trajectories of the target vehicle. Moreover, the fact, that the vehicle's acceleration abilities are less than the deceleration ones is considered

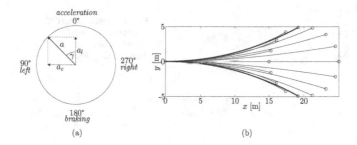

Fig. 2. (a) Kamm's circle. (b) Possible trajectories for a=10 m/s^2, v_0=20 m/s, a prediction of one second [7].

in the computation of possible trajectories. As the calculation of the possible trajectories is based on the state estimation via extended Kalman filtering, the uncertainties of the state estimation, expressed via the covariance matrix P are also accounted for.

Once the maximum possible trajectories are calculated under consideration of state estimation uncertainties, collision parameters, defined according to the GIDAS [6] specification have to be extracted. The algorithm for extracting the collision parameters starts a certain time before the collision and is referenced to the ground truth TTC. Collision parameters are estimated for the main trajectory (i.e. corresponding to the case where the driver takes no action to change the path of the car), as well as for all maximal trajectories. Thus, the predicted collision parameters for the main path, as well as its maximal variation are extracted for further analysis. By comparing the extracted collision parameters with the ground truth, the accuracy of prediction can be analysed.

4 Results

For simplicity and traceability of the results a front-front collision scenario is considered for the analysis. The vehicles are moving towards each other without acceleration. The velocity is varied from 30 km/h to 130 km/h to analyse the effect of velocity on the prediction performance. The prediction starts 500 ms before the ground truth time of collision being stated to be inevitable [4].

The extended Kalman filtering error with and without C2C information in front-front collision scenario for velocities $v_{obj} = v_{ego}$=60 km/h is shown in Figure 3. Additionally, the 3σ confidence interval, obtained from the Kalman filter yielded covariance matrix, is shown. The estimation error is calculated as follows:

$$e_{pos} = \sqrt{e_x^2 + e_y^2} \tag{11}$$

where e_x and e_y are the discrepancies between the position estimation and ground truth position data. The variance of the position estimation is assumed to be equal in both directions. As a confidence interval $3\sigma_x = 3\sigma_y$ has been defined.

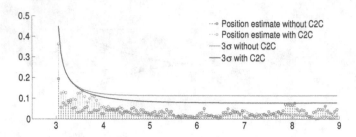

Fig. 3. Position estimation error and 3σ confidence interval for $v_{obj} = v_{ego}$=60 km/h; with and without C2C

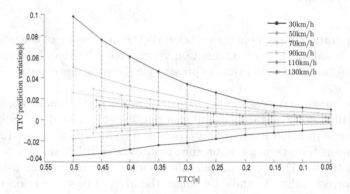

Fig. 4. TTC prediction without C2C information in absence of the measurement noise; $v_{obj} = v_{ego}$

4.1 Time to Collision

Figure 4 presents the estimation of maximal variation of TTC for different velocities without C2C information. Analogously, the case with the use of C2C information for the crash constellation prediction is demonstrated in Figure 5. Hereby 0 denotes the ground truth TTC, and the solid lines present the maximal predicted variation of the TTC, depending on state estimation uncertainty and the driver's interaction can be anticipated earlier due to the immediate transmitted change of the steering wheel. To keep the analysis general the measurement noise is eliminated. Hence, the state estimation is conducted with the same performance in both cases. Therefore, the state estimate is error-free. However, the uncertainty matrix yielded by the Kalman filter, which is involved in the prediction, is the same as if the measurement noise would be present.

Depending on the sensor update rate the prediction may start between [0.5.. 0.45] s before the collision, as it can be seen in Figure 4. Moreover, the figure shows that with an increase in the velocity the variation in TTC prediction is decreasing. This is due to the fact that with higher velocities the minimal turn radius is getting smaller, hence, the trajectories are getting closer. Since the main reason of the collision parameter prediction variation is the driver interaction,

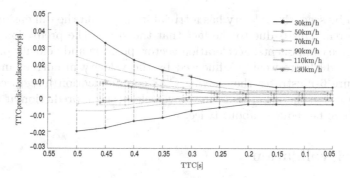

Fig. 5. TTC prediction with C2C information in absence of the measurement noise; $v_{obj} = v_{ego}$

by limited trajectories the prediction variation is lower (Figure 4). As the figure shows, at 500 ms TTC the collision can have a delay up to 100 ms for some crash constellations for $v_{obj} = v_{ego}$=30 km/h. As the vehicle can accelerate less, than decelerate, the collision can take place maximally 35 ms in advance from ground truth TTC in the same case. These values are less by about a factor of five if both object and ego vehicles have the velocity of 130 km/h. The lower the TTC is, the less the TTC prediction varies. Thereby it has to be considered, that for the TTC prediction discrete values are used, thus, sampling noise is present.

4.2   Size of the Prediction Area

The following analysis addresses the size of the prediction area, where the object vehicle's main point is predicted to appear. The size of this area is represented by the half width of it, i.e. the maximum distance in m the vehicle main point can deviate via extreme braking or steering manoeuvres.

The half width of the prediction area without and with C2C information is shown in Figure 6.

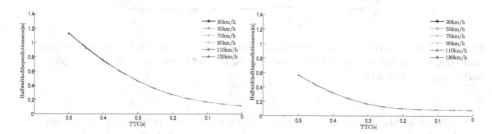

Fig. 6. The half width of prediction area for front-front scenario with and without C2C – left and right respectively

As it can be seen, the velocity has a trivial influence on the dimensions of the prediction area. This is due to the fact that the size of the prediction area depends on three components: acceleration vector, position and velocity prediction uncertainty, which are weakly influenced by the velocity in current implementation. Figure 6 illustrates that having C2C communication integrated to the sensor data fusion the uncertainty in the vehicle position prediction at the time of collision can be reduced about twice.

5   Model Validation

To ensure the realistic and reliable performance of the simulation model, a comparison of the sensor data fusion performance of the simulation model with the real test drive results is made. An overtaking scenario, similar to the one in [1], has been created using the simulation model. Results of the sensor data fusion performance of a test vehicle in an overtaking scenario, presented in [1], has been compared with those from the simulation model. As described in [1], the test drive is performed as follows: driving in the same lane, lane change, acceleration, lane change back, deceleration. The simulation of the overtaking scenario starts with two vehicles in neighbouring lanes, followed by acceleration of the target vehicle, lane change and deceleration. Thus, the time scale of the figures describing the test drive results is different from this of the simulation results. The absolute error in position and velocity estimation in x direction is presented in Figures 7 and 8.

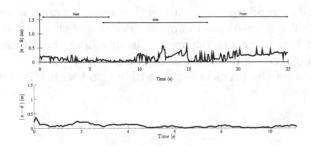

Fig. 7. Absolute error in x position estimation of the test drive (above) [1] and simulation (below) during an overtaking maneuver of the host vehicle with $v_{host} = 80$ km/h and $v_{target} = 90$ km/h

Whereas in the overtaking scenario the test vehicle estimates the target vehicle's velocity with an average error of 0.17 m/s and 0.15 m/s in the x and y directions respectively [1], the simulation model has an estimation error of ~0.15 m/s in both directions. Contrary to the average estimation error of 0.19 m and 0.09 m during the test in the x and y directions accordingly, the simulation model shows a performance of 0.08 m and 0.06 m respectively. This difference can be explained by the abstractions applied to the model. E.g. the assumption that

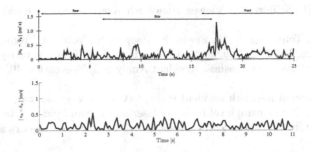

Fig. 8. Absolute error in v_x estimation of the test drive (above) [1] and simulation (below) during an overtaking maneuver of the host vehicle with $v_{host} = 80$ km/h and $v_{target} = 90$ km/h

the ego state is perfectly known leads to a reasonably higher accuracy in the estimations. Nevertheless, better than up-to-date sensors' performance in the simulation model can be justified by the fact that the real life leverage of C2C and its integration to the sensor data fusion would be first possible in several years. At that point more accurate sensors would be available.

6   Conclusion

The present research illustrates the benefits of C2C communication for pre-crash prediction. As it has been demonstrated, the enhancement, which would be achievable through the integration of C2C to the sensor fusion system, is promising. Thereby it is assumed that highly accurate state information about the object can be obtained via the C2C channel. As shown, C2C could bring considerable benefits for the state estimation, which would enhance the collision parameter prediction accuracy. Moreover, the additional information about the driver's current intention (e.g. obtained by steering wheel angle or brake pedal status), available via C2C channel could be used to enhance the crash constellation prediction. The future work concentrates on evaluating different trajectories for active safety systems, as well as improving the constellation prediction algorithm in order to produce a reliable output for active safety measures.

References

[1] Aeberhard, M., Schlichtharle, S., Kaempchen, N., Bertram, T.: Track-to-track fusion with asynchronous sensors using information matrix fusion for surround environment perception. IEEE Transactions on Intelligent Transportation Systems 13(4), 1717–1726 (2012)
[2] Al-Ghamdi, A.S.: Using logistic regression to estimate the influence of accident factors on accident severity. Accident Analysis & Prevention 34(6), 729–741 (2002)
[3] Boufous, S., Finch, C., Hayen, A., Williamson, A.: The impact of environmental, vehicle and driver characteristics on injury severity in older drivers hospitalized as a result of a traffic crash. Journal of Safety Research 39(1), 65–72 (2008)

[4] Braess, H.H., Seiffert, U.: Vieweg Handbuch Kraftfahrzeugtechnik. Springer DE (2011)

[5] Conroy, C., Tominaga, G.T., Erwin, S., Pacyna, S., Velky, T., Kennedy, F., Sise, M., Coimbra, R.: The influence of vehicle damage on injury severity of drivers in head-on motor vehicle crashes. Accident Analysis & Prevention 40(4), 1589–1594 (2008)

[6] GIDAS: German in-depth accident study, http://www.gidas.org

[7] Kaempchen, N.: Feature level fusion of laser scanner and video data for advanced driver assistance systems. Ph.D. thesis, Univ., Fak. fuer Ingenieurwiss. und Informatik (2007)

[8] Karrenberg, S.: Zur Erkennung unvermeidbarer Kollisionen von Kraftfahrzeugen mit Hilfe von Stellvertretertrajektorien. Ph.D. thesis, Technische Universität Carolo-Wilhelmina zu Braunschweig (2008)

[9] Kononen, D.W., Flannagan, C.A., Wang, S.C.: Identification and validation of a logistic regression model for predicting serious injuries associated with motor vehicle crashes. Accident Analysis & Prevention 43(1), 112–122 (2011)

[10] Lee, J., Conroy, C., Coimbra, R., Tominaga, G.T., Hoyt, D.B.: Injury patterns in frontal crashes: The association between knee–thigh–hip (kth) and serious intra-abdominal injury. Accident Analysis & Prevention 42(1), 50–55 (2010)

[11] Nitz, G.: Entwicklung eines Systems zur aktiven Bremsung eines Fahrzeugs in Gefahrensituationen. Ph.D. thesis, Lehrstuhl für Messsystem- und Sensortechnik der Technischen Universität München (2008)

[12] Risch, M.: Der kamm'sche kreis - wie start kann man beim kurvenfahren bremsen. Fahrphysik und Verkehr PdN-Ph. 5/51. Jg. (2002)

[13] Segui-Gomez, M., Baker, S.P.: Changes in injury patterns in frontal crashes: preliminary comparisons of drivers of vehicles model years 1993-1997 to drivers of vehicles 1998–2001. In: Annual Proceedings/Association for the Advancement of Automotive Medicine 46, 1 (2002)

[14] Sobhani, A., Young, W., Logan, D., Bahrololoom, S.: A kinetic energy model of two-vehicle crash injury severity. Accident Analysis & Prevention 43(3), 741–754 (2011)

[15] Tarko, A.P., Bar-Gera, H., Thomaz, J., Issariyanukula, A.: Model-based application of abbreviated injury scale to police-reported crash injuries. Transportation Research Record: Journal of the Transportation Research Board 2148(1), 59–68 (2010)

[16] Wood, D.P., Veyrat, N., Simms, C., Glynn, C.: Limits for survivability in frontal collisions: Theory and real-life data combined. Accident Analysis & Prevention 39(4), 679–687 (2007)

Performance Evaluation of an Ethernet-Based Cabin Network Architecture Supporting a Low-Latency Service

Fabien Geyer[1,2], Stefan Schneele[1], and Wolfgang Fischer[3]

[1] Airbus Group Innovations, Department TX4CP
Willy-Messerschmitt-Str. 1, D-81663 München, Germany
{fabien.geyer,stefan.schneele}@eads.net
[2] Technische Universität München, Institut für Informatik I-8
Boltzmannstr. 3, D-85748 Garching b. München, Germany
[3] Airbus Operations GmbH, Department Cabin Electronic Pre-Development
Lüneburger Schanze 30, D-21614 Buxtehude, Germany

Abstract. Aircraft cabin data network is a key element in today's aircraft, where several functionalities of the cabin are grouped in four different security domains. In todays architectures, each domain is normally separated from the others and uses different standards, ranging from ARINC based standards to customized Ethernet. We present here a future of cabin data network, where the main key principle is the use of a common Gigabit full-duplex Ethernet backbone, shared by all domains. As this new network has to be compliant with existing applications and their requirements, a specific Quality-of-Service (QoS) architecture is investigated in this paper. The contributions of this paper are the description of a new network architecture for cabin networks, and the introduction of a scheduling algorithm called *Time-Aware Deficit Round Robin* (TADRR) enabling an ultra low-latency time-triggered service. We show the benefits of this new architecture via a performance evaluation carried out with the simulator OMNeT++.

Keywords: Cabin Data Network, Low-Latency Service, Scheduling.

1   Introduction

During the last decades, communication networks have become increasingly present in various domains such as industry automation, automotive or avionic systems. One key technology that dominates nowadays the interest of those various domains is Ethernet, as shown in the survey from Sommer *et al.* [21]. While some Ethernet based technologies have been used for almost a decade in avionic systems such as the Avionics Full-DupleX Switched Ethernet (AFDX) technology [8,9], they are generally isolated and dedicated to one part of the complete system. This design where each function has its own system is called Federated Avionics [22]. It has advantages, such as failure isolation, but many drawbacks concerning handling and efficiency.

A. Sikora et al. (Eds.): Nets4Cars/Nets4Trains/Nets4Aircraft 2014, LNCS 8435, pp. 69–80, 2014.

We present in this paper a possible future for the network architecture used in aircraft cabins. This network is based on a shared Ethernet backbone which serves as a common access points to all cabin functions. This new backbone will offer several benefits, among them:

- less cables in the cabin which means a weight reduction for the aircraft,
- use of the well-investigated Ethernet standard which means costs reduction through the use of Commercial Off-The-Shelf (COTS) hardware components,
- introduction of true end-to-end communication in the cabin with well known protocols based on the Internet protocol suite which means the possibility to use solutions already developed for TCP/IP, and introduction of Quality-of-Service (QoS) on the network,
- ability to use standard equipment for logging and testing purpose.

In order to improve part of the end-to-end latency performances, a cut-through forwarding mechanism is used, which means that a frame is forwarded from one port to the other before the whole frame has been received. This mechanism improves the performances of the network as shown later in this paper, and with the help of a time-triggered schedule, it enables an ultra low-latency real-time service. One contribution of this paper is an architecture and a scheduling algorithm called *Time-Aware Deficit Round Robin* (TADRR) designed around this time-triggered scheduling mechanism. This algorithm is in the current trend of designing timing-aware schedulers, as proven by the recent proposal from the IEEE Enhancements for Scheduled Traffic task group [3], with the Time-Aware Shaper.

This paper is organized as followed. We first look at the related work in Section 2. In Section 3, we introduce the new network architecture which will be deployed in future aircraft cabins, the different aircraft security domains supported by this network, as well as some requirements regarding those domains. Then we present in Section 4 our scheduling architecture and algorithm proposition. We then present in Section 5 the performance evaluation of the this network, via simulations done with OMNeT++. Finally Section 6 summarizes and concludes our work, and gives an overview of future improvements.

2   Related Work

The usability of Ethernet based solutions for industrial application is a topic of interest for various industries and has long been studied. Felser presented in [12] a survey of various commercial solutions based on custom Ethernet for achieving real-time communications. A similar study on the history of Ethernet based real-time communications was made by Sauter in [18]. While the first solutions for real-time Ethernet were often based on proprietary technologies, interests have spiked recently with a work effort from the IEEE to standardize a solution for real-time communications. First dedicated to multimedia streams via the IEEE Audio/Video Bridging task group [1], this solution is now being adapted to a wider context via the IEEE Time Sensitive Network task group [4].

Regarding the avionic context, the AFDX technology [8,9] has been success-fully developed as a deterministic Ethernet network. While the benefits of having a deterministic behavior are obvious, it comes at the cost of expensive custom-designed hardware. Research effort has hence been made to asses the suitability of COTS equipments for avionic systems. Performance evaluations of Gigabit COTS Ethernet switches for avionic networks were performed by Meier *et al.* in [17] as well as Jacobs *et al.* [16]. Both studies concluded that the performances in term of latency and jitter are sufficient for avionic applications. A similar study has been made recently by Suen *et al.* in [23], where they focused on the abil-ity to complete the interchange of message between nodes in the system. They also conclude that COTS components provide performances within the range of avionic functions.

While COTS Ethernet solutions are sometimes sufficient, another affordable alternative is to use Field-Programmable Gate Array (FPGA) based solutions, as presented in this paper. As highlighted in the recent work from Carvajal *et al.* in [11], such solution can achieve better service classification and help reduce the end-to-end latency of real-time traffic.

Finally, another solution to reduce the end-to-end latency and jitter is to increase the bandwidths used in the networks. While the majority of the solutions presented in this section are based on 100 Mbps or 1 Gbps, research has also been performed regarding the usability of 10 Gbps Ethernet. With the development of COTS solutions supporting 10 Gbps Ethernet, those solutions were evaluated in the high-performance computing context, such as the work from Feng *et al.* [13], or from Bencivenni *et al.* [10].

3 Cabin Network Architecture

3.1 Topology and Node Description

The Cabin Backbone Architecture is designed in a star/chain architecture, con-sisting of one server in the electronic bay and up to 22 lines through the aircraft cabin. This is depicted in Figure 1. This architecture and topology is similar to the one presented in [14] and [15].

In each line up to 15 network aggregators, with functions similar to Ethernet switches, can be connected in a daisy chain manner, depending on the type of aircraft and its cabin configuration. Throughout the cabin, all devices connect to the network aggregators thus also called *Multi-Domain Network Nodes* (MD-Nodes), as they have the task to bundle the data streams from different functions and security domains onto the single backbone line while ensuring separation of traffic as well as flow control. The latter is especially challenging, as a reliable and fair scheduling for all priorities is required - independently from the position of the network node within the chain.

One specific requirement for this network is that it has to support a real-time service with ultra low-latencies. In this protocol, a packet is transmitted by the server every $31.25\mu s$, and one of the MD-Node has to answer to this packet.

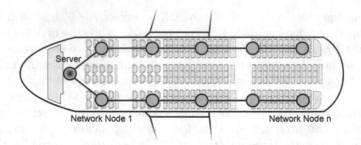

Fig. 1. Cabin Star/Chain Network Topology, here with two lines

The internal architecture of the MD-Node is presented in Figure 2. Three COTS switches are used to aggregate the traffic of each security domain. A special FPGA module is used to schedule the traffic transmitted on the common Ethernet backbone. One specificity of this FPGA is that it uses the principle of cut-through switching, which means that a frame is forwarded from one port to the other before the whole frame has been received. This is opposed to the store-and-forward principle where a frame is forwarded from one port to the other only when the whole frame has been received. A special scheduling architecture (presented in Section 4) is needed in order to prevent the traffic aggregated at this node to interfere with the traffic transmitted on the backbone.

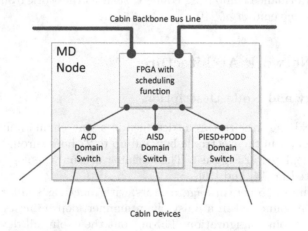

Fig. 2. Architecture of a Multi-Domain Node

3.2   Cabin Network Traffic

According to security aspects all network functions are grouped into domains. Purpose, criticality on the operation of the aircraft, and potential users are criteria for this classification. This follows the definition from [7], where domains are a superset of networks and are an accumulation of related and associated objects.

The arrangement in groups helps to handle functions with similar characteristics, because data flows in the same domain can be treated equal. The aircraft environment ARINC Specification 664 Part 5 [7] distinguishes four domains in which applications share related safety and security aspects:

- Aircraft Control Domain (ACD): all functions which are relevant to control the aircraft.
- Airline Information and Services Domain (AISD): functions to operate the aircraft and airline administrative information for the cabin and flight-crew.
- Passenger Information and Entertainment Services Domain (PIESD): functions relevant to the passenger as infotainment.
- Passenger Owned Devices Domain (PODD): passenger devices which are carried into and used within an aircraft cabin as mobile phones, or laptops. The connectivity to aircraft networks and through these to other services is provided through the PIESD [7].

Along with this traffic, we also defined a special class of traffic called Real-Time Domain (RTD), which has the purpose of scheduling the network access as well as transporting real-time information.

4   Scheduling Architecture

We describe here part of the architecture presented in [14]. This architecture is based on an addressing protocol used for scheduling the access of the MD-Nodes to the backbone, and a specially designed packet scheduler in each MD-Node.

4.1   Addressing Protocol and Real-Time Traffic

As explained earlier, due to the daisy-chain architecture and the routing requirement, the case where one MD-Node overloads a single line has to be prevented. Also, to improve the end-to-end latencies on the network, we use a cut-through mechanism. For this cut-through mechanism to be efficient, the path of a packet needs to be completely congestion free, as otherwise queuing delays may occur. Hence we need a way to avoid those congestions. The solution adopted here is to use a Time-Division Multiple Access (TDMA) architecture, where each MD-Node is allowed to send packets on the backbone only during certain time-slots. In order to avoid the use of clock synchronization protocols to distribute the time-slots, a special network protocol is used, where the server addresses each MD-Node when they are allowed to transmit packets. This protocol is also used to transmit real-time audio data which require the use of the TDMA schedule.

We use here a simple round-robin addressing, where a MD-Node is addressed every $31.25\mu s$, as presented in Figure 3. The length of $31.25\mu s$ is derived from the audio bandwidth of the current Cabin Management System. This means that each MD-Node is allocated a bandwidth of

$$\frac{B_{\text{backbone}} - B_{\text{real-time protocol}}}{\text{number of network node in the line}} \qquad (1)$$

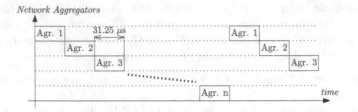

Fig. 3. TDMA with round-robin schedule

and is able to forward packets on the backbone every

$$31.25\mu s \cdot \text{number of network node in the line} \tag{2}$$

4.2 Packet Scheduling: Time-Aware Deficit Round Robin

As a MD-Node is able to forward packets only in its allocated $31.25\mu s$ time-slot, we need to schedule the packet forwarding function. We introduce for this purpose a new packet scheduling algorithm, called *Time-Aware Deficit Round-Robin* (TADRR). It is a variant of the well known Deficit Round-Robin (DRR) scheduler presented in [20]. The original DRR scheduler was designed to be a work-conserving scheduler, which means that the scheduler is idle only when there are not packet available. In our usecase, as packets are not allowed to be forwarded when the MD-Node is not allowed to send, a non work-conserving scheduler is needed. The TADRR scheduler mixes the two following functionalities:

- It is time-aware, meaning that the scheduler respects specific timing where it is allowed to forward packets or not. This is a function currently been developed by the IEEE Enhancements for Scheduled Traffic task group [3], with the so-called Time-Aware Shaper.
- It ensures a fair distribution of the available bandwidth between the different queues or flows.

We define the two following states: `WAIT_SLOT` where the scheduler has to wait for the trigger from the server to be allowed to send, and `ALLOWED_TRANSMIT` where the scheduler is allowed to forward packets. We make the following additions to the dequeuing module from [20]:

- Lines 1 to 5: The maximum allowed packet size is computed using the end of the timeslot (*endTimeslot*) and the current timestamp (t). Note that the Ethernet inter-frame gap (*IFG*) is accounted for.
- Lines 12 and 16 to 19: We use the previously calculated maximum allowed packet size and check it against the head-of-line packet.

Note that as the original algorithm from [20], the complexity of this algorithm is $\mathcal{O}(1)$.

Algorithm 1. Time-Aware Deficit Round Robin - Dequeuing

Dequeuing module:

1: **if** $state \neq$ `ALLOWED_TRANSMIT` **then** return
2: $allowedPacketSize \leftarrow B_{\text{backbone}} \cdot (endTimeslot - t) - IFG$
3: **if** $allowedPacketSize < minEthernetPacketSize$ **then**
4:     $state \leftarrow$ `WAIT_SLOT`
5:     return
6: **while** True **do**
7:     **if** $ActiveList$ is not empty **then**
8:         Remove head of $ActiveList$, say queue i
9:         $DC_i \leftarrow DC_i + Q_i$
10:        **while** $(DC_i > 0)$ and $(Queue_i$ not empty$)$ **do**
11:            $PacketSize \leftarrow Size(Head(Queue_i))$
12:            **if** $PacketSize > allowedPacketSize$ **then** break
13:            **if** $PacketSize \leq DC_i$ **then**
14:                $Send(Dequeue(Queue_i))$
15:                $DC_i \leftarrow DC_i - PacketSize$
16:                $allowedPacketSize \leftarrow allowedPacketSize - PacketSize - IFG$
17:                **if** $allowedPacketSize < minEthernetPacketSize$ **then**
18:                    $state \leftarrow$ `WAIT_SLOT`
19:                    return
20:            **else** break
21:        **if** $Empty(Queue_i)$ **then**
22:            $DC_i \leftarrow 0$
23:        **else** $InsertActiveList(i)$

---

5 Evaluation

We describe here the evaluation of this network which was performed under OM-NeT++ [6] with the INET [5] framework, which includes the required network protocols (Ethernet, IP and UDP). We follow a Monte Carlo method of simulating multiple runs, each time with a different seed and different initialization vector. We use the following assumptions for the simulation:

- All links are set to 1Gbit/s,
- The switch processing time is set to $100\mu s$,
- Queue sizes are set to 1000 packets,
- All the addressing schemes are set to static.

Flows are generated using UDP applications at a fixed bandwidth, but using a uniform distribution for the packet size. The network supports both the real-time protocol, with its $31.25\mu s$ timing, as well as additional applications.

We use the same star/chain architecture as presented in Section 3. We study three topologies presented in Table 1. We define the *uplink* direction as the direction of the packets from a node connected on a line to the central server, and *downlink* direction as the opposite direction. The utilization columns correspond to the portion of the backbone bandwidth that is used.

The results presented here compare two operation modes of the MD-Nodes:

Table 1. Studied topologies

Topology	Configuration		Devices			Utilization (%)	
	Lines	Aggregators	ACD	AISD	PIESD	Downlink	Uplink
1	3	21	18	2	2	15.4	17.4
2	3	21	20	2	2	15.6	13.9
3	4	28	7	1	29	43.7	10.5

- the *cut-through* configuration, which corresponds to the description made in Section 3, with the TDMA schedule and the TADRR packet scheduler;
- the *store-and-forward* configuration, where the FPGA acts as a traditional store-and-forward Ethernet switch, without any considerations for the real-time protocol.

5.1   End-to-End Latency - Real-Time Protocol

We define end-to-end latency as the difference between the moment that the packet has been created in the source device, and the timestamp on which the last bit of the packet is received by the receiving device.

Figure 4 presents the maximum experienced end-to-end latency of the real-time protocol described in Section 4.1. By scheduling appropriately on the cut-through configuration the time when the Ethernet frames of the real-time protocol are sent, we are able to achieve end-to-end latencies below $5\mu s$ for both directions. This is a promising result, as it enables us to have strict feedback loops.

In the store-and-forward configuration, the end-to-end latency is much worse for the real-time protocol. We see here a clear benefit of having dedicated time-slots, where the network is contention free for the real-time protocol.

5.2   End-to-End Latency - Applications

Figure 5 presents the maximum experienced end-to-end latency of the different devices in the topology.

Regarding the downlink direction, we see a definitive benefit in the cut-through configuration. Regarding the uplink direction, we see that the round-robin schedule presented in Section 4.1 is sub-optimal compared to the store-and-forward performances, with almost an order of magnitude of difference. This can be explained by the short time window of $31.25\mu s$ where a MD-Node can only transfer a small number of Ethernet frames. This means that in some cases, packets have to wait multiple round-robin cycles in the MD-Node queue before being able to be transferred.

5.3   End-to-End Jitter Measures

We used the *interarrival jitter* definition from RFC 3550 [19] for our end-to-end jitter measurement. It is defined as the measure of packet arrival time spacing

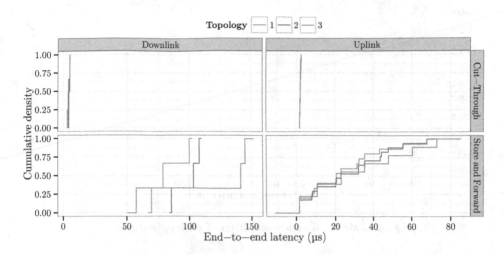

Fig. 4. Maximal end-to-end latency of the real-time protocol

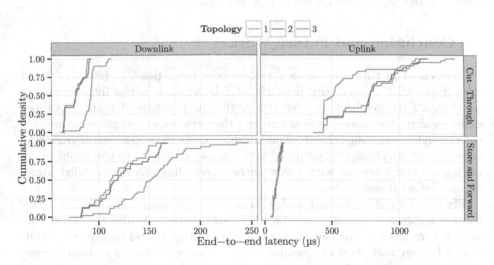

Fig. 5. Maximal end-to-end latency of the applications

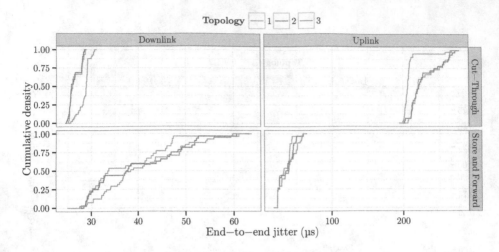

Fig. 6. Maximal end-to-end jitter of the applications

at the receiver smoothed with an exponential filter with parameter 1/16. This definition of the jitter is preferred as only non-spurious deviations in the packet spacing will affect the applications. Figure 6 presents maximum end-to-end jitter experienced by the different devices.

The remarks made for the end-to-end latency also apply for the jitter. We see here again better performances for the cut-through mode in the downlink direction, but worse ones for the uplink direction.

6   Conclusion and Future Work

We presented in this paper a new architecture for a possible future of cabin data network. The main key principle of this network is the introduction of a common Ethernet backbone, shared by the three avionic domains. As those domains share the same physical link and the network aggregators are using a cut-through forwarding scheme, some considerations have to be made regarding access to the backbone. We proposed in this paper a solution to this problem, by mixing a TDMA scheme with a new packet scheduling algorithm called *Time-Aware Deficit Round Robin*.

Via simulations performed with OMNeT++ and its framework INET, we learned some key insights regarding this architecture. While the scheduling architecture has a major benefit on the real-time traffic, and improves the end-to-end latency and jitter of downlink packets compared to the standard store-and-forward configuration, it comes at the cost of large degradations for the uplink performances. The TDMA schedule is the main cause for the good performances of the real-time protocol and the bad performances of the rest of the applications.

We would like to extend our analysis to solutions that may overcome the performance degradations of uplink packets for the non-real-time applications. Regarding the schedule of the different transmissions of the network aggregators, another algorithm than the round robin scheme used here could bring better performances. As some network aggregators produce more bandwidth than other ones, allocating time windows in accordance to this output bandwidth seems logical. This algorithm could work offline, by careful analytical evaluation of the traffic usage at the different points of the network, or online, by extending the real-time protocol described earlier. Finally, we would like to compare the architecture presented here with new advances made by the IEEE 802.1Qbu task group [2], which is currently developing and standardizing frame preemption for Ethernet. This architecture could enable us to completely remove the TDMA schedule while keeping low-latencies for the real-time protocol.

References

1. IEEE 802.1 Audio/Video Bridging Task Group, http://www.ieee802.org/1/pages/avbridges.html (accessed February 25, 2014)
2. IEEE 802.1Qbu Task Group - Frame Preemption, http://www.ieee802.org/1/pages/802.1bu.html (accessed February 25, 2014)
3. IEEE 802.1Qbv Task Group - Enhancements for Scheduled Traffic, http://www.ieee802.org/1/pages/802.1bv.html (accessed February 25, 2014)
4. IEEE Time-Sensitive Networking Task Group, http://www.ieee802.org/1/pages/tsn.html (accessed February 25, 2014)
5. INET Framework for OMNeT++/OMNEST, http://inet.omnetpp.org/ (accessed June 25, 2013)
6. OMNeT++ 4.3 Network Simulation Framework, http://www.omnetpp.org (accessed June 03, 2013)
7. Aeronautical Radio Inc.: ARINC Specification 664P5: Aircraft Data Network, Part 5 - Network Domain Characteristics and Interconnection (April 2005)
8. Aeronautical Radio Inc.: ARINC Specification 664P7: Aircraft Data Network, Part 7 - Avionics Full Duplex Switched Ethernet (AFDX) Network (June 2005)
9. Aeronautical Radio Inc.: ARINC Specification 664P7-1: Aircraft Data Network, Part 7 - Avionics Full Duplex Switched Ethernet (AFDX) Network (September 2009)
10. Bencivenni, M., Bortolotti, D., Carbone, A., Cavalli, A., Chierici, A., Dal Pra, S., De Girolamo, D., Dell'Agnello, L., Donatelli, M., Fella, A., Galli, D., Ghiselli, A., Gregori, D., Italiano, A., Kumar, R., Marconi, U., Martelli, B., Mazzucato, M., Onofri, M., Peco, G., Perazzini, S., Prosperini, A., Ricci, P., Ronchieri, E., Rosso, F., Salomoni, D., Sapunenko, V., Vagnoni, V., Veraldi, R., Vistoli, M., Zani, S.: Performance of 10 Gigabit Ethernet Using Commodity Hardware. IEEE Transactions on Nuclear Science 57(2), 630–641 (2010)
11. Carvajal, G., Wu, C., Fischmeister, S.: Evaluation of Communication Architectures for Switched Real-time Ethernet. IEEE Transactions on Computers 63(1), 218–229 (2014)
12. Felser, M.: Real-Time Ethernet - Industry Prospective. Proceedings of the IEEE 93(6), 1118–1129 (2005)

13. Feng, W., Balaji, P., Baron, C., Bhuyan, L., Panda, D.: Performance Characterization of a 10-Gigabit Ethernet TOE. In: Proceedings of the 13th IEEE Symposium on High Performance Interconnects (Hot Interconnects), pp. 58–63 (August 2005)
14. Fischer, W., Klose, P., Heinisch, M., Reuter, J.: Challenges of Future Cabin Networks. In: Proceedings of Workshop on Aircraft System Technologies, AST (April 2013)
15. Geyer, F., Schneele, S., Heinisch, M., Klose, P.: Simulation and Performance Evaluation of an Aircraft Cabin Network Node. In: Proceedings of Workshop on Aircraft System Technologies, AST (April 2013)
16. Jacobs, A., Wernicke, J., Oral, S., Gordon, B., George, A.: Experimental Characterization of QoS in Commercial Ethernet Switches for Statistically Bounded Latency in Aircraft Networks. In: Proceedings of the 29th Annual IEEE International Conference on Local Computer Networks (LCN 2004), pp. 190–197 (November 2004)
17. Meier, J., Kim, S., George, A., Oral, S.: Gigabit COTS Ethernet Switch Evaluation for Avionics. In: Proceedings of the 27th Annual IEEE Conference on Local Computer Networks (LCN 2002), pp. 739–740 (November 2002)
18. Sauter, T.: The Three Generations of Field-Level Networks - Evolution and Compatibility Issues. IEEE Transactions on Industrial Electronics 57(11), 3585–3595 (2010)
19. Schulzrinne, H., Casner, S., Frederick, R., Jacobson, V.: RTP: A Transport Protocol for Real-Time Applications. RFC 3550 (INTERNET STANDARD), updated by RFCs 5506, 5761, 6051, 6222, 7022 (July 2003)
20. Shreedhar, M., Varghese, G.: Efficient Fair Queuing Using Deficit Round-Robin. IEEE/ACM Transactions on Networking 4(3), 375–385 (1996)
21. Sommer, J., Gunreben, S., Feller, F., Kohn, M., Mifdaoui, A., Sass, D., Scharf, J.: Ethernet - A Survey on its Fields of Application. IEEE Communications Surveys and Tutorials (2), 263–284 (2010)
22. Spitzer, C.R. (ed.): Digital Avionics Handbook. Avionics: Development and Implementation. The Electrical Engineering Handbook Series. CRC Press (December 2006)
23. Suen, J., Kegley, R., Preston, J.: Affordable Avionic Networks with Gigabit Ethernet: Assessing the Suitability of Commercial Components for Airborne Use. In: Proceedings of IEEE Southeastcon 2013, pp. 1–6 (2013)

Aeronautical Ad Hoc Network for Civil Aviation

Quentin Vey[1], Alain Pirovano[1], José Radzik[2], and Fabien Garcia[1]

[1] ENAC, 7 avenue Édouard Belin, CS 54005 31055 Toulouse Cedex 4, France
[2] Université de Toulouse/ISAE, 10 avenue Édouard Belin, BP 54032,
31055 Toulouse Cedex 4, France

Abstract. Aeronautical communication systems are constantly evolving in order to handle the always increasing flow of data generated by civil aviation. In this article we first present communication systems currently used for en-route aircraft. We then propose Aeronautical Ad hoc NETwork (AANET) as a complementary communication system and demonstrate its connectivity and assess the throughput by simulations based on real aircraft trajectories over the French sky and over the Atlantic ocean.

1 Introduction

Since the beginning of civil aviation, communications have always relied on direct link communication. As the traffic and the needs for safety grew, new technologies have been developed and implemented.

The airline traffic is expected to grow continuously in the coming years. This, combined with the migration from analog to digital and the new applications should lead to a saturation of the current communication systems capacity by 2020 [1].

The majority of data traffic in civil aviation application is observed between one aircraft and the ground. That's why new air-ground communication systems are expected. In this article, we propose AANET (Aeronautical Ad hoc Network) as an in-flight communication system to allow aircraft to communicate with the ground, in complement to other existing or future in-flight communication systems.

This paper is organized as follow: in section 2 we present some specificities of civil aviation communications, in section 3 the currently available communication systems are described as well as our proposal. This proposal is evaluated in section 4 and in section 5 our current research axes are given.

2 Civil Aviation Communication Specificities

In this section we present some properties and specificities of civil aviation communications.

A. Sikora et al. (Eds.): Nets4Cars/Nets4Trains/Nets4Aircraft 2014, LNCS 8435, pp. 81–93, 2014.

2.1   Airspace Properties

The upper airspace is almost exclusively used by commercial aircraft in cruise flight ("en-route" traffic). In the context of our study, we don't take into account the regulatory differences between airspaces in this section but focuses instead on the mobility patterns. We consider the two following zones:

- **Continental:** The continental traffic is generally characterized by numerous different routes, and a high aircraft density (especially above western Europe).
- **Oceanic:** As shown in Fig. 1, in oceanic area (and in remote continental area) the aircraft trajectories follow a limited set predefined routes, and aircraft density is low compared to continental airspace. In this case the aircraft traffic is similar to the cars traffic on a highway: the vehicles follow almost the same path, with similar speeds.

   We consider here the particular case of the North Atlantic Tracks (NAT). These tracks define the routes followed by aircraft flying between Europe and north America. They are updated every day according to weather conditions in order to minimize fuel consumption and flight duration.

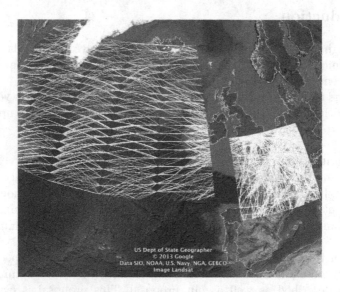

Fig. 1. Tracks of oceanic and continental traffic over 24 h

2.2   Civil Aviation Communication Classification

Four categories of communications are defined in the annex 10 of the International Civil Aviation Organization (ICAO) [2] regarding their safety level.

- **ATSC:** Air Traffic Services Communication (critical). This class regroups communication between pilot and ATC to ensure the safety, speed and efficiency of the flight.
- **AOC:** Aeronautical Operation Control (critical). "Communication required for the exercise of authority over the initiation, continuation, diversion or termination of flight for safety, regularity and efficiency reasons"[2]. Used by airline companies to communicate with aircraft (e.g. maintenance messages, fuel levels, exact departure and arrival time...).
- **AAC:** Aeronautical Administrative Control (non critical). "Communications necessary for the exchange of aeronautical administrative messages"[2]. AAC are neither linked to the security nor the efficiency of the flight. A few examples of AAC are informations regarding passengers (list of passengers, connections), special cleaning requests , hotel booking for flight attendants....
- **APC:** Aeronautical Passenger Communication (non critical). Examples of such communication are VoIP, e-mail, web browsing.

It has to be noted that critical communications follow very stringent international rules defined by ICAO (for example only some dedicated frequency band can be used) and are based on dedicated systems. These latter must meet very specific QoS requirements (transaction time, continuity, availability, integrity). These regulatory constraints does not apply to non critical communications, even if they may have to meet some requirements according to the applications (e.g. delay for passenger VoIP).

The current solution in civil aviation communication to ensure segregation is a physical segregation between critical communications and non-critical communications. The equipments aboard aircraft are physically different.

We will focus only on systems dedicated to critical services (ATSC, AOC) in the rest of this paper.

3   Proposal of a Communication System

3.1   Civil Aviation Data Link Communication Systems

Data link communication are used since the early 80's. We list here some technologies currently used by civil aviation to communicate with en-route aircraft, and some technologies foreseen to be deployed in a near future.

Cellular Systems. Cellular systems provide a direct link between the aircraft and a ground station. With the exception of the HFDL, all these cellular systems are limited to a line-of-sight (or lower) range, thus requiring the deployment of a large ground infrastructure to cover a region and unable to cover oceanic flights far from the shores. The offered capacity is shared between all aircraft within range of ground station. Moreover, for VDL there is a need for handover procedure generally based on ground comunication sytem between stations.

Despite these drawbacks, they offer a reliable service at lower cost than satellite-based systems, and are suitable for numerous continental flights.

Existing and Future Cellular Systems.

- **HFDL:** High Frequency Data Link. Standardized in 1999, it offers a link capacity up to 1.8 kbit/s [3] (shared between every aircraft within range of a station). Because of the unique propagation of the HF radio a single station can cover a very large area (range is usually around 2500 km, can go up to 4000 km depending on ionospheric conditions). This very long range enables a global coverage (including polar areas) using only 14 stations. The major drawback of this system is its low capacity.
- **VDL mode 2:** VHF Data Link. Specified in 1996 by the ICAO, it offers a 31.5 kbit/s capacity [3] and a line-of-sight coverage (400 km).
- **L-DACS:** L-DACS is foreseen by the Single European Sky ATM Research (SESAR) project as a new data link communication systems, expected in 2016. It should operate in L-band and offer a 200 kpbs capacity.

Satellite-Based Systems. Satellite systems offer a link between two transceivers (an aircraft and a control center for example) by using satellites as relay. A satellite-based systems provides wide coverage and relatively high speed links, but at the expense of a high cost. Main types of satellites are:

- **GEO:** Geostationary Earth Orbit. A satellite on GEO appears on a fixed position in the sky and covers one third of the Earth. The drawback of this position are high delays due to the distance, and a lack of coverage of the polar regions. It has also to be noted that the integration of a high-gain antenna (required for high-speed connections) on an aircraft is a complex and costly task.
- **LEO:** Low Earth Orbit. A satellite on LEO will have a lower delay and can cover polar regions, but will appear moving in the sky, thus requiring a whole constellation to enable a continuous coverage.

Existing and Future Satellite-based Systems.

- **Inmarsat:** InmarSat is a GEO satellite operator and a communication service provider, providing connection from 1.2 kbit/s to 10.5 kbit/s for critical services (Aero L and Aero H/H$^+$ products).
- **Iridium:** Iridium provides communications using LEO satellites, offering 2.4 kbit/s links.
- **IRIS:** SESAR project has defined an GEO satellite solution in partnership with the European Space Agency (ESA) called IRIS, the operational solution is expected in 2020. The offered capacity should be several dozens of kbit/s.

Conclusion on Existing and Future Communication Systems. Table 1 summarizes the main properties of these systems currently used or in development for critical applications in civil aviation. However the traffic growth and the new expected applications should saturate these current communication systems by 2020 [1]

We would like to underline the offered capacity and covered areas. These values are indeed quite unsual for most ground network where high capacity means often several Mbps, and must be kept in mind when studying the performances of communication systems designed for civil aviation critical communications.

In this context, communications during oceanic flights (or over remote continental areas) implies that the aircraft is equipped with at least the only two currently available communication systems for critical communications, which are the more often for this area HFDL and satellite link. Furthermore above polar regions (latitude higher than 70°) the only satellite system available is Iridium.

Table 1. Summary of the performances of several communication systems for civil aviation

System	Offered capacity	range / coverage	currently operational
HFDL	1.8kbit/s per ground station	2500 km	yes
VDL mode 2	31.5 kbit/s per ground station	400 km	yes
L-DACS	200 kbit/s per ground station	400 km	no (under test)
InmarSat aero L	1.2 kbit/s per aircraft	for lat. under 70°N/S	yes
InmarSat aero H/H$^+$	10.5 kbit/s per aircraft	for lat. under 70°N/S	yes
Iridium	2.4 kbit/s per aircraft	global	yes
IRIS	dozens of kbit/s per aircraft	for lat. under 70°N/S	no (expected 2020)

3.2 AANET as a Civil Aviation Communication System

In this context, particularly in oceanic airspace, we propose AANET as a new complementary solution to send messages from the aircraft to the ground. The main expected advantage is that, an aircraft could send/receive a message to the ground even if no ground station is in line of sight.

Others expected advantages at this step of the study are the following:

− Simple and relatively light ground infrastructure required,
− Simple and relatively light embedded system,
− Redundancy of the path in the network particularly when aircraft density is high (multipath).
− Load-balancing ability when several path are available.

Nevertheless AANETs present several issues. For instance, the connectivity relies on aircraft density in the considered airspace and the direction from aircraft to the ground will result in a tree logical topology in which ground gateways or on some parts of the network may represent bottlenecks.

3.3 Proposed Architecture for Access Layers

The AANET architecture we propose implements omnidirectional radio links between the different nodes with two types of links: a2a (aircraft to aircraft) and a2i (aircraft to infrastructure or ground stations), with a bandwidth of 20 MHz in the 2 GHz band (actual frequency will depend on radio spectrum availability). To manage concurrent accesses to the media three allocation methods have been considered: by frequency (Frequency Division Multiple Access, FDMA), by time (Time Division Multiple Access, TDMA) and by spreading code (Code Division Multiple Access, CDMA). Combinations of these methods are possible. However, frequency division cannot share the available bandwidth in the considered topology without significantly reducing the available bandwidth for every connection. And time division raises an important issue on clock synchronization. Therefore, we propose the use of Direct Sequence CDMA (DS-CDMA), a solution also used in 3G mobile, networks and proposed in IRIS [4]. DS-CDMA has the major advantage that it does not require any coordination between nodes and it allows multiple simultaneous transmissions. The collisions which occur can be resolved in the receiver thank to the low intercorrelation between two different and well chosen spreading codes. It has to be noted that this collision recovery can only be done within the limits of Multiple Access Interferences (MAI). This represents the major limiting factor of the performance of CDMA systems. This particular point has been investigated in [5]

4 Feasibility and Performance Assessment

4.1 Connectivity Assessment

Related Work. Previous studies on AANET, for example the ATENAA [6] project and NewSky project [1] and [7], have studied the feasibility of an ad-hoc network. [1] and [7] are focused on the connectivity of airplanes over the North Atlantic Tracks by assuming that the aircraft took off and landed at scheduled time and followed the shortest path (geodesic trajectory) between departure and arrival airport. They conclude to the feasibility of a such network. However, as shown in Fig. 2, differences as high as 1000 km are observed between real trajectory and shortest path. Also, the eastbound and westbound traffic do not follow the same tracks at all: aircraft flying from Europe to America tend to follow a route going several hundreds kilometers north of the shortest path in order to avoid the jet-stream, a high-altitude powerful wind blowing eastward.

Fig. 2. Difference between the shortest path trajectory (green) and the real trajectory (red) for a Paris-New York flight on the 16th of September 2011

Methodology. In order to avoid this bias, our study is based on the replay of real traffic traces from the French civil aviation authority and Eurocontrol based on either radar data or position report from the aircraft itself. If a time-scale smaller than the one provided by the reports is required, intermediate positions are interpolated between these reported positions. In the rest of this paper, we will refer to these as "pseudo-real" positions.

Because of these datasets, our study focus on the north Atlantic (for oceanic traffic) and French (for continental traffic) airspaces. For the continental study, the ground stations have been placed near air traffic control centers, and for oceanic airspace they have been positioned on the coasts and islands along the tracks.

Connectivity has been assessed with a software we have specifically developed, AeRAN (for Aeronautical Ad hoc Networks). It processes the datasets presented in the previous paragraph and a list of ground stations, then gives several statistics as output such as the amount of aircraft connected to the ground, the ratio of aircraft connected directly or via several aircraft to a ground station. In this part, because only the connectivity is being evaluated, computations are made under the assumption that links are ideal, i.e. it is possible to send data to any aircraft within a given range without interference.

Results. The software presented in the previous part has been used to compute the number of aircraft connected to a ground station (directly or through a multi-hop path) in function of the time of day for several link ranges (100, 200 and 400 km). The results are presented in Fig. 3.

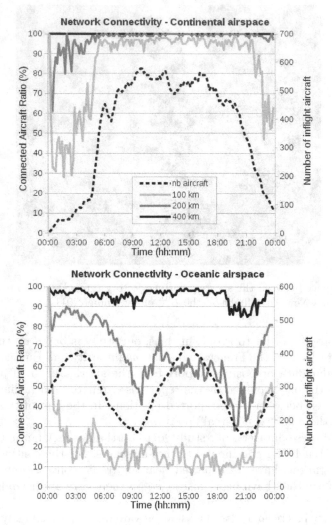

Fig. 3. Communication range influence on network connectivity

These results underline the influence of the communication range on the aeronautical ad hoc network connectivity (solid lines and left y axis) in the considered continental airspace and oceanic airspace. As expected, the connected aircraft ratio increases with the communication range up to a point. And after this point increasing communication range does not have significant impact on connectivity. These figures, on which the number of instantaneous flying aircraft has been displayed (dotted lines and right y axis), let also think that the this number and connectivity are correlated. We can see here that in the French sky a communication range of 150 km allows a mean connectivity of 90 % of the aircraft during the day, with 99 % of aircraft connected between 6:00 and 21:00. But in the oceanic airspace, this communication range should be 350 km in order to ensure a mean connectivity greater than 90 % in the day. These latter results are explained by the fact that the aircraft density is lower in the oceanic airspace. It is important here to note again that aeronautical ad hoc networks have to be considered more as an additional mean for air-ground communication than as an alternative stand-alone one. Hence, these results let us foresee the benefits of this solution particularly considering its low cost relatively to other solutions.

4.2 Throughput Assessment

Methodology. TCP propose several functionalities and mechanisms to fairly adapt its sending rate to the network available capacity. So we use this transport protocol in a "reno-like" version in order to assess the effective mean offered capacity to each aircraft in the AANET . We have developed a simulation model for aeronautical ad hoc network with OPNET Modeler (Riverbed), which is a discrete event simulator for all kind of networks. The aim of the model is to simulate aeronautical ad hoc network in a realistic way. Aircraft positions are defined using the same method and inputs data as in our homemade tool AeRAN as explained in section 4.1. Considering physical layer properties the capacity of each inter nodes link is set to 1 Mbit/s.

To determine the available throughput per aircraft, a path to the ground station has to be chosen for each of them. At this step, we use the shortest path, regarding the distance between the nodes, to the closest ground station given by the Dijkstra algorithm. Thus we obtain a list of edges representing the path from each aircraft to the ground station. The maximum distance to establish a connection between two aircraft (their communication range) is a simulation parameter. We used the link ranges that produced a mean connectivity of 90 % found in the previous part (350 km for oceanic, 150 km for continental). We also made the hypothesis that there were enough spreading codes available for every aircraft. However, link interferences for simultaneous transmissions are taken into account in this part.

At each time of the simulation, we consider a graph whose nodes are aircraft and ground stations, and whose edges are the available connections between them. We assume that a connection is always available between all pairs of ground stations (based on a ground network infrastructure). The weight of each edge in the graph is its length. Then, the Dijkstra algorithm is used to find in this graph the shortest path from each aircraft to a ground station. It gives for each connected aircraft a path to the closest ground station. Finally, considering the application level, as the idea is to assess the available throughput for each aircraft, we use greedy TCP sources in our model. Such TCP sources generate new TCP segments as soon as the previously sent ones are acknowledged. Hence, data are generated at the highest possible rate regarding the aeronautical ad hoc network congestion and the obtained results indicates the expected throughput that could be achieved by each aircraft.

Results. Table 2 shows the mains results obtained after a simulation campaign. The

Table 2. Shortest path routing results

	Mean aircraft throughput kbit/s	Max delay (95 % pkts) ms	Mean delay ms
Continental	38,3	551	401
Oceanic	68,2	426	184

These quite better throughput performances in oceanic airspace are mainly explained by the fact that, in the considered oceanic airspace, the ratio between the number of ground stations and the number of aircraft is better. Actually there are a maximum of about 400 simultaneous flying aircraft (with a mean of 275 aircraft) for 8 ground stations during one day. Comparatively, in the French sky, our case study for continental area, the PIAC (Peak Instantaneous Aircraft Count) is near 600 aircraft with a mean of 500 simultaneous flying aircraft between 6:00 and 21:00 for 5 ground stations.

Hence, we can see that, in this worst-case scenario (TCP greedy) with a very simple routing algorithm and a basic Reno-like TCP congestion control algorithm, AANET performs better than any currently operational system for critical communications in terms of throughput per aircraft.

4.3 Assessment with a Realistic Application

As an example of realistic application, we consider one proposed by the BEA (in English: Bureau of Inquiry and Analysis for Civil Aviation Safety) which is the French authority responsible for safety investigations into accidents or incidents in civil aviation. The main objective of this application is to make easier data recovery from flight recorders by periodically sending flight parameters to the ground in oceanic airspace. Three sets of parameters which should be sent each second for a given aircraft have been defined [8]. The bulkier set has a size of 12,288 bits. So we created a specific model in a new scenario which allows each aircraft to behave as if it sends a set of flight data of 12,288 bits each second. Of course this type of traffic source exhibits higher burstiness than the one used in the previous sections. The simulation results show that all packets reach successfully the ground station. The maximum observed delay for 95 % of packet is 178 ms. The proposed innovative communication system is therefore compatible with such a realistic application.

5 Further Work

5.1 Disruption Tolerance

Regarding the speed of airliners, the topology of AANET is highly dynamic, particularly in the considered continental airspace. A single aircraft or a sub-set may be temporarily disconnected from the rest of the AANET. Some little disruptions may not be considered as full disconnection, depending on the maximum tolerated end to end delay for our applications. For a given link range, a disruption tolerance should increase connectivity, and for a given connectivity, these tolerated disruptions should allow to lower the transmission power, thus reducing interferences and increase throughput.

The dynamicity of the network topology is currently being assessed with the software presented in 4.1 and the same "pseudo-real" trajectories in order to evaluate the improvement offered by the tolerated disruptions. Depending on the results of this study, Disruption/Delay Tolerant Network (DTN) [9]) ability will be considered to improve connectivity. The DTN paradigm makes a network robust to high delays or disruptions by taking advantage of the movement of the nodes to improve connectivity.

5.2   CDMA Code Allocation

In the throughput study we assumed that there were enough spreading codes of a given length for every aircraft and that a given code was statically assigned to each aircraft, which is a simplification of our problem. In reality the spreading code attribution algorithm should be adaptive, distributed, enable spatial reuse of codes and give the shortest possible code for every link in order to maximize link throughput. The codes themselves also must allow this. Orthogonal Variable Spreading Factor (OVFS) are a family of spreading codes that meets these requirement by providing orthogonal spreading codes of different length, i.e. codes of different length which enable concurrent transmission.

Jiang et Al. proposed in [10] an interesting code attribution algorithm. It is based on a RTS/CTS mechanism with spreading code negotiation on a signaling channel, then a data transfer with the negociated code. During the negotiation, each node evaluates the required length of the spreading code based on the network activity in his neighborhood. It has been tested with simulated aircraft movement and must now be tested with our "pseudo-real" aircraft traffic data. We are also working on some improvement of this algorithm that have to be implemented and assessed.

5.3   Investigation of Different Routing Algorithms

We used in this paper a very simple routing algorithm (shortest geographic distance). In the rest of our research, we plan to investigate routing algorithms based more advanced metrics. For example, the following metrics seems interesting to choose the routing path:

- Number of relays: minimizing the number of relays should reduce the total processing delay and the collision.
- Link durability: a higher link durability could also be preferred in order to reduce the amount of disconnections. In this case, link stability can be evaluated with Doppler frequencies: a lower Doppler frequency between two aircraft means that their trajectories (speed and heading) are similar and that the link is less likely to be interrupted.

– Network load: because an AANET will offer several different routes (depending on aircraft density), the routing algorithm could perform load balancing by choosing routes according to the load of the relay nodes.

Of course, combinations of these metrics and others are possible.

Clustering is also another solution that could enhance the AANET performances. To build clusters one can use the same metrics as the one presented above, for example [11] uses similarities in the trajectories in order to create long-lasting clusters.

Several routing algorithms from the MANET and the VANET communities uses these metrics and should be considered for AANETs (similarities between VANET and MANET have been studied in [12], e.g. TOPO [13], DSR [14] , GPSR [15], MUDOR [16]. AANET specific routing algorithm have also been proposed, e.g. ARPAM[16], GLSR[17], AeroRP[18].

Unfortunately, performances of these routing algorithms are rarely assessed with real aircraft trajectories. In our further work we will test the most interesting ones with simulations based on the "pseudo-real" trajectories presented in 4.1.

6   Conclusion

Considering traffic growth, new expected applications and the limitation of existing systems, new communication systems will be needed for civil aviation in the future, especially for oceanic flights. In this article we proposed AANET as a complement to the cellular and satellite communication systems. Our study demonstrates that its throughput performance are sufficient to cope with current and some new applications. However its connectivity is heavily dependent on the aircraft density. But, because it performs better when aircraft density is high, AANET can relieve other communication systems that would otherwise be overloaded under these conditions.

We end this paper with some research axes that will be investigated in our further works in order to improve the overall performances of air ground communication based on AANET.

References

1. Schnell, M., Scalise, S.: Newsky - concept for networking the sky for civil aeronautical communications. IEEE Aerospace and Electronic Systems Magazine 22(5), 25–29 (2007)
2. International Civil Aviation Organisation. ICAO annex 10 (November 2005)
3. ICAO annex 10, vol. 3 (July 2007)
4. Indra. Antares communication standard design definition file. Technical note IRIS-AN-CP-TNO-610-ESA-C1, ESA, DRL Nr: D020 (September 2013)
5. Besse, F., Pirovano, A., Garcia, F., Radzik, J.: Interference estimation in an aeronautical ad hoc network. In: 2011 IEEE/AIAA 30th Digital Avionics Systems Conference (DASC), pp. 4C6–1–4C6–11 (October 2011)

6. Amirfeiz, M.: ATENAA project: Advanced technologies for networking in aeronautical applications. In: Aerodays 2006, Vienna (June 2006)
7. Medina, D., Hoffmann, F., Ayaz, S., Rokitansky, C.-H.: Feasibility of an aeronautical mobile ad hoc network over the north atlantic corridor. In: 5th Annual IEEE Communications Society Conference on Sensor, Mesh and Ad Hoc Communications and Networks, SECON 2008, pp. 109–116 (June 2008)
8. BEA. transmission declenchee de donnees de vol (triggered flight data transmission). Technical report, Bureau d'Enquètes et d'Analyses pour la sécurité de l'aviation civile (March 2011)
9. Ali, S., Qadir, J., Baig, A.: Routing protocols in delay tolerant networks - a survey. In: 2010 6th International Conference on Emerging Technologies (ICET), pp. 70–75 (October 2010)
10. Jiang, Z., Zhou, M.: Spread spectrum MAC protocol with dynamic rate and collision avoidance for mobile ad hoc network. IEEE Transactions on Vehicular Technology 56(5), 3149–3158 (2007)
11. Fan, W., Shi, Y., Chen, S., Zou, L.: A mobility metrics based dynamic clustering algorithm for VANETs. In: IET International Conference on Communication Technology and Application (ICCTA 2011), pp. 752–756 (2011)
12. Royer, M., Pirovano, A., Garcia, F.: Survey on context-aware Publish/Subscribe systems for VANET. In: Berbineau, M., Jonsson, M., Bonnin, J.-M., Cherkaoui, S., Aguado, M., Rico-Garcia, C., Ghannoum, H., Mehmood, R., Vinel, A. (eds.) Nets4Cars/Nets4Trains 2013. LNCS, vol. 7865, pp. 46–58. Springer, Heidelberg (2013)
13. Wang, W., Xie, F., Chatterjee, M.: An integrated study on mobility models and scalable routing protocols in VANETs. In: 2007 Mobile Networking for Vehicular Environments, pp. 97–102 (2007)
14. Johnson, D., Hu, Y., Maltz, D.: rfc4728: Dynamic source routing (February 2007)
15. Karp, B., Kung, H.T.: Gpsr: Greedy perimeter stateless routing for wireless networks. In: Proceedings of the 6th Annual International Conference on Mobile Computing and Networking, MobiCom 2000, pp. 243–254. ACM, New York (2000)
16. Karras, K., Kyritsis, T., Amirfeiz, M., Baiotti, S.: Aeronautical mobile ad hoc networks. In: 14th European Wireless Conference, EW 2008, pp. 1–6 (June 2008)
17. Medina, D., Hoffmann, F., Rossetto, F., Rokitansky, C.-H.: A geographic routing strategy for north atlantic in-flight internet access via airborne mesh networking. IEEE/ACM Transactions on Networking 20(4), 1231–1244 (2012)
18. Peters, K., Jabbar, A., Cetinkaya, E.K., Sterbenz, J.P.G.: A geographical routing protocol for highly-dynamic aeronautical networks. In: 2011 IEEE Wireless Communications and Networking Conference (WCNC), pp. 492–497 (2011)

A DDS-Based Middleware for Cooperation of Air Traffic Service Units

Erwin Mayer and Johannes Fröhlich

Offenburg University of Applied Sciences,
Faculty of Electrical Engineering & Information Technology, Offenburg, Germany
{erwin.mayer,johannes.froehlich}@hs-offenburg.de

Abstract. Air traffic is by nature crossing borders and organizations. The supporting infrastructure represents a federative distributed system of independent Air Traffic Service Units, typically each with its own proprietary system architecture. Interaction between the centers is taking place over dedicated protocols, often organized as a mesh of 1:1 bilateral data exchanges.

This contribution gives an overview of the ongoing efforts to standardize this data exchange. At the core is a data-centric view, using a shared virtual Flight Object as the IT counterpart of a real flight. It permits a uniform way to access and update a flight's static and dynamic attributes. A middleware is presented that implements this abstraction and maps it onto a physical level, employing DDS (Data Distribution Service) technology for the 1:N dissemination of flight data.

Keywords: Air Traffic Control, Data Distribution Service (DDS), distributed systems, data replication, middleware, standardization.

1   Introduction

An aircraft, between departure and landing, typically crosses a large number of different areas of responsibility, each implemented by an individual Air Traffic Service Unit (ATSU) such as airports, approach control centers or en-route centers. Each of these ATSUs is based on a complex proprietary technical infrastructure, maintaining the counterpart of the physical aircraft flight in the form of a proprietary IT data record that is being updated along the progress of the flight [1].

Once an aircraft leaves the air space of a given center, a transfer to the neighboring ATSU is initiated, often accompanied by a telephone transfer of the respective air traffic controllers or by the use of 1:1 coordination protocols like OLDI (Online Date Interchange) [2]. In the neighboring center, upon notification of the prospective arrival of an aircraft, another IT data record is constructed and maintained, comprising similar attributes for the given flight, however again in a proprietary representation and often with an equipment vendor-specific set of services to interact with this representation.

Though this federative approach of ATSU organization has in the past demonstrated its effectiveness in terms of safe operation around the world, it is not ideal.

A. Sikora et al. (Eds.): Nets4Cars/Nets4Trains/Nets4Aircraft 2014, LNCS 8435, pp. 94–102, 2014.

First, because there are multiple representations of the same physical object, there may be varying views of a flight in terms of its detailed attributes and the time that they are updated [1]. For example, while a neighboring ATSU may be informed about the exact arrival time and transfer altitude at the time of transfer, a ATSU further downstream, e.g. the arrival airport, may not be immediately aware of this data and possibly cannot anticipate implicit delays.

Second, a large number of 1:1 interactions between ATSUs may need to take place, in order to communicate and agree changes in a flight plan, like the re-routing of a flight due to conditions at the arrival airport.

The air traffic control community is for many years aware of this situation [1][3][4]. As part of large research programs like SESAR (Single European Sky ATM Research Programme) [3], the harmonization and standardization of air traffic control technology and procedures is ongoing.

This contribution describes standardization activities in the domain of center cooperation and presents a prototype middleware implementation, DDS-ATC (Data Distribution System for Air Traffic Control) taking into account results of this standardization. DDS-ATC provides a data-centric approach to the problem: Instead of the use of multiple 1:1 interactions between ATSUs operating on proprietary IT data records, it employs a single representation of a flight in the form of a shared virtual Flight Object (VFO). It is virtual because there exists no single physical storage location for it. It is shared, because all ATSUs, secured by access rights, can equally access it for reading and modification over a set of standardized services.

Chapter 2 gives an overview of the standardization efforts in this domain. Chapter 3 introduces the middleware's architecture and functional scope, while chapter 4 gives some details about the project environment, followed by a summary (chapter 5).

2   Ongoing Standardization Efforts

The main goal of ongoing standardization is to provide a common interface for all air traffic service participants and a data format in which the flight information is unambiguously described and exchanged.

Initial ideas in this area were discussed in [1]. Based on this and other general developments (e.g. [3]), during recent years several standard initiatives, driven by U.S. and European aviation authorities, have been in place. These include the Flight Object Interoperability Proposed Standard (FOIPS) [5], the Flight Object Interoperability Specification (ED-133) [5] which is itself based on FOIPS, and the Flight Information Exchange Model (FIXM) [6]. All three proposals are still under development with a large number of still open issues.

- The FOIPS Standard [4] prepared by EUROCAE (European Organisation for Civil Aviation Equipment) and introduced in 2005 is one of the first standardization efforts in this domain. It includes both a data model defining flight objects and additional rules for exchanging this flight object data. The "analysis model" uses UML to define the data structure and states of flight objects. The "usability model" describes textually how the service participants should interact under various roles. A

Flight Object Server (FOS) is the system instance used for providing access to the network and exchanging the flight objects. FOIPS does only take care of the service interface between the FOS and the application layer and not between the FOSes themselves. Therefore there are no architectural limitations for further specifications.

- Based on FOIPS another standard initiative, the ED-133 [5], was raised by EUROCAE in 2009. The ED-133 replaces the FOIPS specification and delivers a more comprehensive requirement analysis and specification for the exchange of flight data. Unlike the FOIPS specification, the ED-133 covers only civilian aviation and focuses on the FOS interface to ensure interoperability for implementations of different vendors. On communication level DDS [7] is suggested for distributing the Flight Object data among the participants. Web services enable a parallel request/response-based communication scheme between single nodes. XML is proposed as encoding for the data payload.
- On the other side of the Atlantic, the FAA went a slightly different approach introducing the FIXM [6] model in 2012. FIXM focuses on the flight object data format and is by intent not defining a protocol. Based on the ISO19100 guidelines FIXM enables compatibility to existing EUROCONTROL standards like the Aeronautical Information Exchange Model (AIXM) and the Weather Information Exchange Model (WXXM). FIXM comprises a "Foundations Package" comprising basic data types, a "Core Package" defining flight attributes, and a "Message Package", for meta-data how to encapsulate Core Data for exchange (however no corresponding protocol). All data is foreseen to be XML-encoded. Another useful feature of FIXM is the core/extension structure which allows a dynamic adaption of the data model.

Currently it is not clear in which direction the standardization is further going. Therefore it is important to gather experience through implementations like DDS-ATC, which prototype this type of flight data exchange.

3   DDS-ATC Middleware

3.1   Architectural Model

The initial goal of the DDS-ATC prototype development was to provide a universal ATSU exchange service based on the concept of a virtual flight object on the basis of DDS transport. As part of the DDS-ATC requirement analysis the available standards described in chapter 2 were evaluated and compared. It was decided to take an approach that would not block going for either of the proposals. Figure 1 describes the architectural model for the DDS-ATC, which is in line with the FIXM [6], FOIPS [4] and ED133 [5] proposals.

The chosen architecture is such that it can support both the FIXM and the FOIPS/ED133 type of flight data. On the protocol level it takes onboard suggestions from the ED133 [5] proposal.

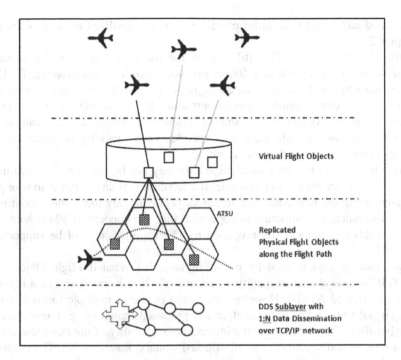

Fig. 1. Architectural Model

On top of the hierarchy in Fig. 1 are the physical aircraft. For each aircraft there exists a corresponding virtual flight object (VFO), composed of a large number of data attributes describing the details of the flight. Updates are triggered by air traffic controllers or automatic processes in the Flight Data Management Processes (FDMP) of the ATSUs. The VFO is created ahead of departure and has a lifetime at least until the aircraft has landed or departed the supervision area.

While it would be ideal to physically implement the VFO on a central server, this forbids itself, mainly for safety reasons. Instead, a replicated approach is used, where each ATSU interested in a given flight (these are at least those centers that control the airspace along the flight path) store a copy of the VFO in form of a PFO (Physical Flight Object). In order to keep the PFOs consistent, a replication control protocol is required (see below).

The update of a VFO must include the update of all related PFOs (i.e. physical replica). This is effected by using OMG's DDS (Data Distribution Service) [7], as suggested in [5], over a well secured TCP/IP provider network.

3.2 Virtual Flight Objects

A VFO is composed of a number of static and dynamic attributes. Example of static attributes may be the flight identification, departure airport or available onboard equipment. Dynamic attributes include the flight's SSR code (dynamic radar-based identification), its position, trajectory, flight path or arrival time. A VFO's attributes are specified and stored in a platform independent, standardized manner as discussed in chapter 2.

While FOIPS [4] and FIXM [6] rely on the use of a trajectory (i.e. a tracker-derived sequence of recent and future positions that a flight passes), ED133[5] proposes the additional use of a shared flight script, which comprises all control instructions (e.g. a climb command) and constraints that determine the current and future path of a flight. By additionally sharing this information each ATSU can compute its own trajectory of the flight and is not dependent on the validity and accuracy of the trajectory computation of a previous center [5].

It may be the case that an individual ATSU may not be capable to decide upon a change to a VFO by itself. For example, if a re-routing of an aircraft is to take place, the centers along the new path have to agree. While already today there exist procedures and technical infrastructure to cope with this, the concept of VFOs lends itself to support this requirement. As proposed by [5], negotiation shall be supported on VFO level.

Negotiation is implemented by means of so-called What-If Flight Objects (WI-FOs). WIFOs have the same quality as normal VFOs, i.e. are stored in a replicated way on all affected ATSUs. However, they exist in one or multiple forms in parallel to the original VFO and include the effects of proposed changes (e.g. a new route).

The benefit of this approach is the immediate availability of the complete attribute set of a new air traffic situation at all affected centers. Based on WIFOs, controllers can decide, whether they agree with the change, make counterproposals (in form of updates to the WIFOs) or may reject a proposal (deletion of WIFO), leaving the original VFO unchanged. In case of acceptance by all related ATSUs the WFO is transformed to a VFO.

3.3 Replication Approach

While [6] only provides a data model without a concrete protocol, [5] proposes a replication scheme on top of an underlying transport. This chapter describes the role of replication and its implementation in the DDS-ATC middleware.

While the use of replication in distributed systems has a long history and is well understood (e.g. summary [10]), an adaptation to the specific air traffic control scenario is required.

As sketched in Fig. 1, the physical flight objects implementing a VFO are not stored at all participating ATSUs, but only on a subset of "interested" nodes. Typically this includes the centers along the flight path of an aircraft, and possibly some individual neighboring centers. Thus replication is partial and dynamic.

Fig. 2 rehashes the principle problem of updates in such an environment. Due to delays of the underlying network inconsistent views of the stored data and optionally an inconsistent state of the replica may result. In the example, two ATSUs controlling adjacent airspace of a specific aircraft update the flight's VFO by sending 1:N messages to all nodes hosting a PFO. Due to differing network latency, the updates arrive in a different order (A→B, B→A) at some of the other ATSUs, resulting in potentially different end states.

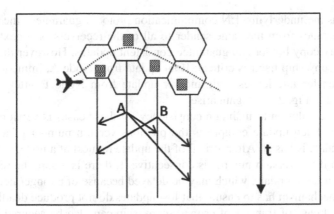

Fig. 2. Inconsistent Update Order as part of 1:N Distribution

In the case of node failures and recovery, further inconsistencies may result: For example, a recovering node may receive a mixture of (replayed) recovery messages from neighboring nodes and live messages for an active flight. Again a proper order of updates has to be ensured. Finally, a recovering node must be prevented itself from contributing to other nodes, while its state is not yet complete.

At the core of the replica update issue lies the uncontrollable latency of the network and the fact that updates can be triggered independently by different ATSUs. The approach taken in DDS-ATC for solving this problem is to use a variant of a Primary Copy Replication Control (PCRC) algorithm. The approach follows the ED133 [5] requirement analysis and specification.

General PCRC algorithms are well-understood (see e.g. [10]). In their core, they assume that one of the replicas assumes a distinguished role: Updaters always direct their request to the primary copy, which then synchronizes the updates to the other (secondary) copies. For the given context the standard PCRC is adapted in the following ways:

1. Instead of having a single node in the network acting as primary copy holder (which would be not acceptable from the safety point of view), the granularity of the primary-copy-ship is chosen to be a single flight. At a given point in time, for two distinct flights typically two differing ATSUs host the respective primary copy. This caters for a strong independence and resilience against failures.

2. The primary-copy-ship is not static but transferred between ATSUs dynamically: Each time the operational responsibility for a flight changes (e.g. an air traffic controller transfers a flight to the neighboring sector), implicitly on the level of the DDS-ATC middleware a transfer of primary-copy-ship is effected. The middleware receives notification of such a transfer over its API from the FDMP, and triggers a token transfer message, that is broadcast (1:N) to interested ATSUs. From now on the new token holder coordinates the update.

As long as the underlying 1:N communication protocol guarantees the ordered delivery of messages from the same sender to all of the receivers (see next chapter), a single primary copy holder can guarantee consistent updates. However the transfer of the primary-copy-ship itself is critical: If an update from Node A, immediately before the token transfer interleaves with another update from Node B after the transfer, situations like in Fig. 2 may again arise.

The selected solution to maintain consistency for these cases is version numbering for the PFOs. Each update comprises the previous version number of a PFO, upon which the update is based. After arrival of the update request at a node, it will only be implemented if the version number is consecutive. If there is a gap, the receiver must wait for the missing update, which may be delayed because of a longer network route. (A timeout mechanism has to ensure that lost updates do not produce deadlocks.)

The critical case of transfer of primary-copy-ship can also be secured by this mechanism: the current version number of PFO is itself conveyed as part of the token transfer message. Because the new primary holder continues to use this value, the synchronization at the reception side is guaranteed.

3.4   DDS Transport

In order to physically distribute PFO updates around the network an underlying transport protocol is required. OMG's DDS (Data Distribution Service) middleware [7] is used for this purpose. It offers a natural data-centric approach, permitting data types of the exchanged application objects to be defined as part of an IDL (Interface Definition Language). This follows the approach taken in CORBA (Common Object Request Broker Architecture) [9] and caters for flexibility and extensibility requirements of the given application. Flight objects are mapped onto DDS topics, which are maintained using a general Publish/Subscribe paradigm [11].

The following are rationales for the use of DDS as part of the project's middleware:

1. DDS implements a 1:N type of data transport and makes use of underlying Layer 3 multicast functionality, if available. This caters for a high efficiency, required in particular to cater for physical data replication.
2. DDS offers fine-grained QoS (Quality of Services) attributes for its services. Both reliable and best effort data transfer are possible, and are employed for different types of user data. Deadline monitoring (both towards the network and towards the service consumer) is used for peer- and self-supervision.
3. The DDS provider system can be configured to work in an entirely peer-to-peer manner, i.e. without central storage or broker, mandatory for the given environment, with its independent ATSUs.
4. Further benefit of using DDS as a lower layer relate to its realtime performance characteristics: The DDS stack is optimized for realtime transfer of data with a low computational overhead and a lean message exchange service. [14]

Next to the standardization of the API (application programming interface) [7], DDS also provides a "wire protocol", i.e. a unique specification of how data is exchanged, such that different nodes can use different DDS supplier stacks [8].

There is a fairly large amount of user experience in mission critical software available for DDS ([12],[13]), promising successful application to the DDS-ATC middleware.

4   Project Environment

The DDS-ATC middleware project is funded by a federal grant from the German ministry of commerce (BMWI) and is executed together with an industry partner from the air traffic control technology sector.

Target operating system for the system is LINUX (CentOS). Development environment is Eclipse using C++ as programming language. PostgreSQL is used as the database management system for storing the PFOs.

On the networking side four DDS candidate implementations have been evaluated as part of separate work ([12]): OpenDDS, RTI DDS, OpenSplice and CoreDX. Based on its combination of provided functionality, standard compatibility and licensing conditions, the community version of OpenSplice [13] was selected as the platform for the DDS-ATC middleware. It offers core functionality needed for VFO implementation on an open source basis.

5   Conclusion and Future Work

This paper presented a middleware approach for the cooperation of a regional federation of air traffic control centers taking into account newer standards of the air traffic control community ([4],[5],[6]). It could be shown that the abstraction of one Virtual Flight Object per aircraft, implemented on top of a replication-based distributed physical storage, caters for both: a simple, uniform access to the data by all players, as well as an efficient standardized exchange of data over a wide area network. For the latter, it could be shown, that the DDS transport vehicle can be tailored in a favorable way to the specific project requirements.

The DDS-ATC project is still ongoing. A base system is operational and shows good initial results concerning performance and stability. As future work of the project a simulation environment for DDS-ATC will be developed that in particular allows to carry out performance tests and to inject errors on networking or application level for system testing of the final application.

References

1. Hill, A.: The Flying Object: A Flight Data Management Concept. In: IEEE A&E Systems Magazine, pp. 11–18 (2004)
2. Eurocontrol: On-Line Data Interchange (OLDI), EUROCONTROL-SPEC-106, Ed. 4.2 (2010), ISBN 978-2-87497-061-0, http://www.eurocontrol.int/publications
3. Sesar (Single European Sky ATM Research) Programme, Joint Undertaking Site (2013), http://www.sesarju.eu

 4. EUROCONTROL: Flight Object Interoperability Proposed Standard (FOIPS), Study D7 Revision 1.04 (2006), http://www.eurocontrol.int/services/foips
 5. EUROCAE, EuropeanOrganisation for Civil Aviation Equipment: Flight Object Interoperability Specification, Standard ED-133 (2009), http://www.eurocae.net
 6. Federal Aviation Authority (FAA): Flight Information Exchange Model (FIXM), Rev. 2.0 (2013), http://www.fixm.aero/content/fixm-core-releases
 7. Open Management Group: Data Distribution Service for Real-time Systems, Standards specification document V 1.2 (2007), http://www.omg.org/spec/DDS/1.2/
 8. Open Management Group: The Real-time Publish-Subscribe Wire Protocol, DDS Interoperability Wire Protocol. DDS-RTPS standard specification V2.1 (2010), http://www.omg.org/spec/DDS-RTPS/2.1/
 9. Open Management Group: CORBA (Common Object Request Broker) Architecture (2012), http://www.omg.org/spec/CORBA
10. Tanenbaum, A., Van Steen, M.: Distributed Systems, Principles and Paradigms, pp. 273–320. Prentice Hall International (2007)
11. Eugster, et al.: The Many Faces of Publish/Subscribe. ACM Computing Surveys 35(2), 114–131 (2003)
12. Mayer, V.: Evaluation of the DDS Publish/Subscribe Standard and application to an Air Traffic Control Scenario. Master Thesis, Hochschule Offenburg (2013) (in German)
13. Schmidt, D.C., van't Hag, H.: Addressing the Challenges of Mission-Critical Information Management in Next-Generation Net-Centric Pub/Sub Systems with OpenSplice DDS. In: Proceedings of the 2008 IEEE International Parallel & Distributed Processing Symposium, IPDSP 2008, Miami, pp. 1–8 (2008)
14. Bliesner, S., Comitz, P., Sweet, D.: Enhancing the Distribution of Radar Surveillance Data. In: Integrated Communications, Navigation and Surveillance Conference, ICNS 2008, pp. 1–8 (2008)

Reliability Analysis of ZigBee
Based Intra-Vehicle Wireless Sensor Networks

Md. Arafatur Rahman

Department of Electrical Engineering and Information Technologies (DIETI)
University of Naples Federico II, Naples, Italy
Laboratorio Nazionale di Comunicazioni Multimediali (CNIT), Naples, Italy
arafatur.rahman@unina.it

Abstract. Reliability is one of the key issues in intra-vehicle wireless sensor networks, which is a promising research area due to the increasing demand of various safety and convenience applications in the vehicle. Most of the works about this mainly focus on wireless, sensor and computer networks. However, the reliability analysis on intra-vehicle wireless sensor networks is not similar to others because of the complex environment created by a large number of parts inside the vehicle. In this paper, we analyse the reliability for single link between a base station and a sensor node based on ZigBee standard. A robust system design can be achieved by utilizing the experimental analysis.

1 Introduction

The number of sensors in the vehicle has increased significantly due to the various safety and convenience applications. Generally, the Sensor Nodes (SNs) and the microprocessor in a vehicle communicate over a serial data bus are connected with physical wires. The wired architecture is not scalable and flexible due to the internal structure of the vehicle [1]. Therefore, there is an increasing level of appeal to design a system in which the wired connections to the SNs are replaced with wireless links. To this end, the feasibility of different technologies, such as Radio Frequency IDentification (RFID) and ZigBee, has been investigated in [2–5].

Reliability is one of the key issues in Intra-Vehicle Wireless Sensor Networks (IVWSNs). The level of reliability varies with different communication parameters such as distance between Base Station (BS) and SN, transmission power and channel fading. From Fig. 1, we can see that the transmission power of the BS is set P_{t1} if the distance between BS and SN is d_1. When the distance is increased from d_1 to d_2 then the transmit power needs to be increased from P_{t1} to P_{t2} for receiving same level of received signal by the SN. We also notice that due to the increasing of distance between BS and SN, the obstacles may come in the propagation path that changes the line-of-sight (LOS) to non LOS (NLOS). As a result, the fading distribution of a channel will be changed. For achieving the reliability in IVWSNs, the above parameters need to be adjusted.

A. Sikora et al. (Eds.): Nets4Cars/Nets4Trains/Nets4Aircraft 2014, LNCS 8435, pp. 103–112, 2014.
© Springer International Publishing Switzerland 2014

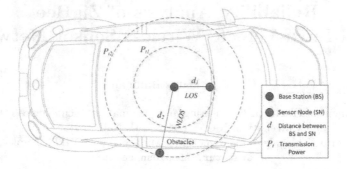

Fig. 1. Communication parameters change the scenario inside the vehicle

In this paper, we analyse the level of link reliability in IVWSNs based on ZigBee standard, with the objective to achieve a robust system design by utilizing the experimental outcomes.

The rest of the paper is organized as follows. In Section 2, we provide the related work, while in Section 3, we describe the theoretical background. In Section 4, we discuss about the reliable link analysis between BS and SN. Finally, in Section. 5, we conclude the paper.

2   Related Works

Most of the works about reliability analysis mainly focus on wireless, sensor and computer networks [8–15]. However, few works have addressed particularly the link reliability in Intra-Vehicle Wireless Sensor Networks [1, 5, 7, 16–18]. In [8], the authors present an empirical study based link reliability estimation in wireless networks. In [9], the author proposes an approach which especially overcomes the drawback of Monte Carlo method for only solving reliability problems in large computer networks. In [10], the authors improve the paper [9] and make it suitable for the WSNs. The reliability analysis on intra-vehicle communication is not similar to the aforementioned works due to the the internal structure of the vehicle. In [1], the authors report the statistical characteristics of 4 representative intra-vehicle wireless channels on the basis of the results of received power measurements and verify the level of reliability of the channels. In [5], the authors evaluate the ZigBee standard specially for cyber-physical systems, which is a class of engineered systems that features the integration of computation, communications, and control. Finally, in [7], the authors propose another work to characterize the wireless channel for intra-vehicle wireless communication.

Unlike all the aforementioned works, in this paper we analyse the level of link reliability in IVWSNs and tune the communication parameters based on ZigBee standard. A robust system design can be achieved by utilizing the experimental results.

3   Theoretical Background

This paper analyses the reliability of intra-vehicle wireless sensor networks. In this section, we provide the theoretical background of the work.

The time variations of the received power are usually caused by the changes in the transmission channels due to the fading effects. There are two kinds of fading: i) large-scale fading and ii) small-scale fading.

Large-scale fading includes path losses and shadowing effects. The path loss is generally modeled through empirical evaluations specially for WSN. The expression of path loss can be written as follows [6]:

$$PL(d)[dB] = PL(d_0)[dB] + 10\gamma \log_{10}(\frac{d}{d_0}) + X_\sigma \tag{1}$$

where X_σ is a Gaussian random variable, $\mathcal{N}(0, \sigma^2)$, with zero mean and variance σ^2, also known as log-normal shadowing, $PL(d_0)$ is the path loss in dB at the reference distance d_0 and γ is the path loss exponent.

The performance of this model not only depends on the distance between transmitter and receiver, but also the path loss exponent and the variance of the log-normal shadowing.

On the other hand, small-scale fading is caused by the interference between multiple versions of the transmitted signal, which arrive at the receiver at slightly different times. Three different propagation mechanisms can happen between the antennas of the transmitter and receiver in the vehicle such as reflection, diffraction and scattering [1]. Reflection occurs when the signal impinges on objects whose dimensions are larger than λ (signal wavelength). Diffraction occurs when the signal impinges on objects with sharp edges. Scattering occurs when the signal impinges on several objects whose dimensions are smaller than or comparable to λ.

The fading distributions of wireless channels can be characterized into two distribution functions, such as Ricean and Rayleigh distributions. The Ricean distribution occurs when there is a presence of dominant stationary signal component, such as a line-of-sight propagation path. In this case, the random multipath components arriving at different angles are superimposed on a stationary dominant signal. Because of the large number of multipath components, central limit theorem can be applied and the sum of these random components can be approximated by the Gaussian distribution. The Ricean distribution is given by:

$$p(r) = \frac{r}{\sigma^2} e^{-\frac{r^2 + A^2}{2\sigma^2}} I_0(\frac{Ar}{\sigma^2}) \tag{2}$$

where r is the received signal amplitude, A is the peak amplitude of the stationary dominant signal, and $I_0(.)$ is the modified Bessel function of the first kind and zero-order.

On the other hand, the Rayleigh distribution occurs, when the dominant signal becomes weaker and comparable to other random multipath components. The Rayleigh distribution is given by:

$$p(r) = \frac{r}{\sigma^2} e^{-\frac{r^2}{2\sigma^2}} \tag{3}$$

The Ricean distribution can be described in terms of a parameter K which is defined as the ratio between the deterministic signal power and the variance of the multipath and is given by [1]:

$$K[dB] = 10 \log(\frac{A^2}{2\sigma^2}) \tag{4}$$

The Rayleigh distribution can be considered as a special case of the Ricean distribution with $K = -\infty$.

It could expect that the intra-vehicle wireless channels with strong LOS signals to follow the Ricean distributions while the others NLOS signals to follow the Rayleigh distributions. However, these conventional ideas may not work properly, due to the complex environment created by a large number of parts inside the vehicle. Consequently, the actual distributions need to be obtained by analyzing the experimental data, as discussed in [1, 7].

In this paper, we analyse the level of link reliability in intra-vehicle wireless sensor networks with the varying of communication parameters, which are suitable for IVWSNs. The reliability for single link is defined as follows:

Definition 1 (Reliability for single Link). *The level of reliability for single link between a BS and a SN depends on the function of Throughput, Packet Loss Ratio (PLR) and Valid Packet (VP).*

where the parameters of the function are defined as follows:

Definition 2 (Throughput). *Throughput is the total data traffic (bits/s) successfully delivered to the 802.15.4 MAC layer of the receiver and sent to the higher levels.*

Definition 3 (Packet Loss Ratio). *Packet Loss Ratio (PLR) is the ratio of Dropped Packets (DPs), i.e., packets that are affected by a number of bit errors and can not be corrected by the Cyclic Redundancy Check (CRC), and Arrived Packets (APs), i.e., packets arriving at the BS with a power greater than the receiver sensitivity.*

Definition 4 (Valid Packet). *Valid Packet (VP) is the percentage of packets that arrive at the receiver with power greater than the receiver sensitivity.*

4   Reliable Link Analysis between BS and SN

In this section, we study about the communication reliability on single link between BS and SN, since the design of a IVWSNs can not be separated from the study on the link between the different sensor nodes distributed in the vehicle. In order to do that, we have carried out a series of simulations through a discrete event simulation software, OPNET, with the relative packages for the ZigBee module.

4.1   Scenario

A pair of transmitter (i.e., SN) and receiver (i.e., BS) communicates each other within a vehicle. The BS collects the packets that are transmitting periodically by the SN. The BS and the SN are placed at a distance d.

4.2   Communication Parameters

The following are the communication parameters that are used for the experiments.

- Transmit Power set: {-10, -15, -20, -25} dBm, which is suitable for ZigBee, such as the Crossbow MICAz MPR2400 [19];
- Carrier frequency: 2.4 GHz (ISM band), which is used on ZigBee sensor node;
- Receiver sensitivity: The reception threshold of the BS is set equal to -95 dBm, typical for ZigBee [19];
- Distance between BS and SN: 1 to 6 meters (with intervals of 1 meter), which will cover the entire length (or more) of a passenger car;
- Transmission Period: 10 ms;
- Channel: The channels 1 (a, b) are for NLOS paths with Rayleigh fading. The channels 2 (a, b) are for LOS paths with Rice fading and the value of the parameter K is 20.16 dB and 16.08 dB, respectively. The path loss exponent γ for channel 1(a) and 2(a) is 3 and for channel 1(b) and 2(b) is 4. The values of shadowing deviation $\sigma[dB]$ is 8. These values are suitable for intra-vehicle wireless sensor networks [1, 7].
  Packet size: 220 bits (ZigBee packet header 120 bits + data 100 bits);
- Parameters MAC: Retransmissions have been disabled in order to focus on the quality of the connection;

4.3   Experimental Results

In this subsection, we discuss the reliability analysis between BS and SN in terms of throughput, Packet Loss Ratio (PLR) and Valid Packet (VP), as described in Definition 1-4.

In terms of throughput, we analyse how the average throughput behaves with the variation of distance between BS and SN, transmission power, and also the effect of Rice and Rayleigh fading.

Fig. 2 shows the behavior of the average throughput with the variation of distance between BS and SN for Channel 1 (a, b). The figure clearly shows a decreasing trend of the average throughput with increasing distance. The cause of this trend is due to the low power level of the packets arriving to the antenna of BS. Indeed, from (1) we know that the path loss increases with distance and the effect of the log-normal shadowing involves a fluctuation in time of the received power, which can further degrade the performance of the communication. These fluctuations may lead the level of received power below the receiver sensitivity (-95 dBm). Then, the BS evaluates the received packet as noise and consequently, the packet is lost.

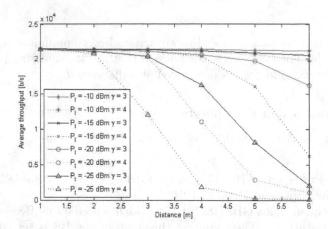

Fig. 2. Comparison of the average throughput experienced by the Channel 1 (a, b)

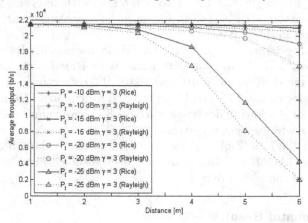

Fig. 3. Comparison of the average throughput experienced by the channel 1(a) and 2(a)

In Fig. 3, it shows the comparison of the average throughput experienced by the channel 1(a) (Rayleigh fading) and 2(a) (Rice fading). From the figure, we see that, as expected, the channel 2 (a) is the favorable case because of the presence of dominant signal component in Rice fading. We also (as similar in Fig. 2) note that a dramatic decrease of average throughput when the distance between BS and SN passes from 4 to 5 meters, in the case of Rice fading with -25 dBm, it is about 12 Kb/s, while in the case of Rayleigh fading, it is about 8 Kb/s. This trend is due to the decreasing of received power below the receiver sensitivity.

In terms of PLR, we analyse how the PLR behaves with the variation of distance between BS and SN, and transmission power, as shown in Fig. 4. The PLR increases with the increasing of distance between BS and SN. As the distance increases, the power level at which packets are received by the BS decreases, and

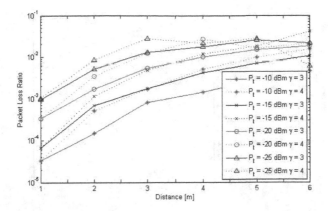

Fig. 4. Packet loss ratio versus distance between BS and SN

consequently, it decreases the SNR. This causes the increasing of the BER that may discard the packets. We note that, for low values of the transmission power, for example $P_t = -25\ dBm$ with $\gamma = 4$, and $P_t = -20\ dBm$ with $\gamma = 4$, seem to improve the performance, as in Fig. 4 one can observe a decrease of PLR. In fact, this trend is not for the improvement of performance, but the fact is the number of packets arriving at the BS, with a low power than the receiver sensitivity, increases to this point that distorts the performance, as the PLR is calculated from the packets arriving at reception with a power greater than the receiver sensitivity. In the case of Rice fading, the PLR can be considered equal to zero, since the performance in terms of Bit Error Rate (BER) are very good so that there is no packet discarded after the error control check CRC.

In terms of VP, we analyse how the VP behaves with the variation of distance between BS and SN, transmission power, and also the effect of Rice and Rayleigh fading.

Fig. 5 shows the percentage of valid packets for channel 1 (a, b), the function of the distance between BS and SN, and for different transmission power. As expected, the figure shows a decreasing trend with the distance, Similar to Fig. 2, the cause of this trend is due to the low power level of the packets arriving to the antenna of BS.

In Fig. 6, it is shown the comparison of valid packets experienced by the channel 1(a) (Rayleigh fading) and 2(a) (Rice fading). Similarly in Fig. 3, the channel is affected by Rayleigh fading provides the worst performance with respect to Rice fading. The difference of the valid packets in two cases is more noticed by increasing the distance between BS and SN; in fact, within 3 meters of distance the performance are almost same. This trend can be explained by considering that multipath effects are as more as the difference between the propagation paths; obviously, the less is the distance between transmitter and receiver, the less will be the propagation paths and the distance between them will be decreased.

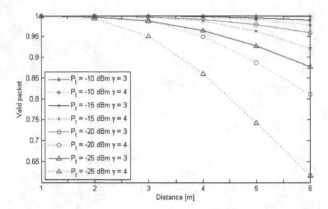

Fig. 5. Comparison of valid packets experienced by the Channel 1 (a, b)

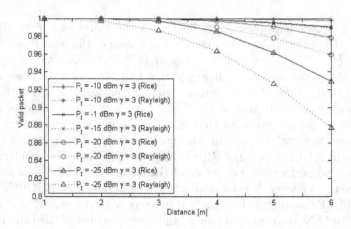

Fig. 6. Comparison of valid packets experienced by the channel 1(a) and 2(a)

From the above analysis, it can be concluded that the BS should be placed in the center of the vehicle specially for the less transmission power. In the hostile scenario (where fading = Rayleigh, $\gamma = 4$, $\sigma = 8$ dB, $P_t = -25$dBm, distance between BS and SN = 2m), the level of reliability is: 97% of the maximum achievable throughput, PLR $< 10^{-2}$ and 99% of VP. In the less hostile scenario (where fading = Rice, $\gamma = 3$, $\sigma = 8$ dB, $P_t = -25$dBm, distance between BS and SN = 3m) the level of reliability is: 97.2.3% of the maximum achievable throughput, PLR is zero and 99% of VP. In the considered scenario (where fading = Rayleigh/Race, $\gamma = 3/4$, $\sigma = 8$ dB, $P_t = -15$ dBm, distance between BS and SN $< 4m$) the level of reliability is: 98.5% of the maximum achievable throughput, PLR is 1.2 x 10^2 and 99% of VP. Indeed, the performance will be more better while the power will increase, however the life time of the SN will be reduced. In the future work, we will investigate the performance by introducing the concept of cognitive radio in intra-vehicle wireless sensor networks [20–23].

5 Conclusion

In this paper, we analyse the reliability for single link between a BS and a SN based on Zigbee standard. Furthermore, we study the hostile and less hostile scenario for analyzing the link reliability. Finally, we consider the suitable scenario for reliable link in the intra-vehicle wireless sensor networks. A robust system design can be achieved by utilizing this experimental analysis. In the future work, we will investigate the performance by introducing the concept of cognitive radio in intra-vehicle wireless sensor networks.

Acknowledgments. This work is partially supported by the project "Mobile Continuos Connected Comprehensive Care (MC3CARE), "DRIVEr monitoring: technologies, methodologies, and IN-vehicle INnovative systems for a safe and ecocompatible driving (DRIVE IN^2)" founded by the Italian national program Piano Operativo Nazionale Ricerca e Competitivit 2007-2013 and the project, "Sviluppo di Tecniche di Comunicazione di Sistemi Embedded Distribuiti" founded by POR Campania FSE 2007/2013.

References

1. Tsai, H.M., Viriyasitavat, W., Tonguz, O.K., Saraydar, C., Talty, T., Macdonald, A.: Feasibility of In-car Wireless Sensor Networks: A Statistical Evaluation. In: Proc. IEEE SECON, pp. 101–111 (2007)
2. Tonguz, O.K., Tsai, H.M., Saraydar, C., Talty, T., Macdonald, A.: Intra-car wireless sensor networks using RFID: Opportunities and challenges. In: Proc. INFOCOM MOVE Workshop, pp. 43–48 (2007)
3. Tsai, H.M., Tonguz, O.K., Saraydar, C., Talty, T., Ames, M., Macdonald, A.: Zigbee-based intra-car wireless sensor networks: A case study. IEEE Wireless Commun. 14, 67–77 (2007)
4. Niu, W., Li, J., Liu, S., Talty, T.: Intra-vehicle ultra-wideband communication testbed. In: Proc. MILCOM, pp. 1–6 (2007)
5. Xia, F., Vinel, A., Gao, R., Wang, L., Qiu, T.: Evaluating IEEE 802.15.4 for Cyber-Physical Systems. EURASIP Journal on Wireless Communications and Networking (2011)
6. Akyildiz, I.F., Vuran, M.C.: Wireless Sensor Networks. Wiley (2010)
7. Moghimi, A.R., Tsai, H.M., Saraydar, C.U., Tonguz, O.K.: Characterizing IntraCar Wireless Channels. IEEE Transactions on Vehicular Technology 58, 5299–5305 (2009)
8. Woo, S., Kim, H.: Estimating Link Reliability in Wireless Networks: An Empirical Study and Interference Modeling. In: Proc. INFOCOM, pp. 1–5 (2010)
9. Shpungin, Y.: Network with Unreliable Nodes and Edges: Monte Carlo Lifetime Estimation. International Journal of Applied Mathematics and Computer Sciences 4, 168–173 (2007)

10. Jin, Y.L., Lin, H.J., Zhang, Z.M., Zhang, Z., Zhang, X.Y.: Estimating the Reliability and Lifetime of Wireless Sensor Network. In: Proc. 4th International Conference on Wireless Communications, Networking and Mobile Computing (WiCOM), pp. 1–4 (2008)

11. Xing, B., Mehrotra, S., Venkatasubramanian, N.: RADcast: Enabling reliability guarantees for content dissemination in ad hoc networks. In: Proc. IEEE INFO-COM, pp. 1998–2006 (2009)

12. Cacciapuoti, A.S., Calabrese, F., Caleffi, M., Di Lorenzo, G., Paura, L.: Human-mobility enabled wireless networks for emergency communications during special events. Elsevier Pervasive and Mobile Computing 9, 472–483 (2013)

13. Cacciapuoti, A.S., Calabrese, F., Caleffi, M., Di Lorenzo, G., Paura, L.: Human-mobility enabled networks in urban environments: Is there any (mobile wireless) small world out there? Elsevier Ad Hoc Networks 10, 1520–1531 (2012)

14. Caleffi, M., Paura, L.: M-DART: Multi-path Dynamic Address RouTing. Wireless Communications and Mobile Computing 11, 392–409 (2011)

15. Cacciapuoti, A.S., Caleffi, M., Paura, L.: A theoretical model for opportunistic routing in ad hoc networks. In: Proc. of IEEE SASN 2009: The International Workshop on Scalable Ad hoc and Sensor Networks, S. Petersburg (RU), October 11-12 (2009)

16. Ma, X., Zhang, J., Yin, X., Trivedi, K.S.: Design and Analysis of a Robust Broadcast Scheme for VANET Safety-Related Services. IEEE Transactions on Vehicular Technology 61, 46–61 (2012)

17. Xu, Q., Mak, T., Sengupta, R.: Vehicle-to-vehicle safety messaging in DSRC. In: Proc. ACM Int. Workshop VANET, Philadelphia, PA, pp. 19–28 (2004)

18. Xing, B., Mehrotra, S., Venkatasubramanian, N.: RADcast: Enabling reliability guarantees for content dissemination in ad hoc networks. In: Proc. IEEE INFO-COM, pp. 1998–2006 (2009)

19. MPR/MIB mote hardware users manual, http://www.xbow.com

20. Cacciapuoti, A.S., Caleffi, M., Paura, L., Savoia, R.: Decision Maker Approaches for Cooperative Spectrum Sensing: Participate or Not Participate in Sensing? IEEE Transactions on Wireless Communications 12, 2445–2457 (2013)

21. Rahman, M.A., Caleffi, M., Paura, L.: Joint path and spectrum diversity in cognitive radio ad-hoc networks. EURASIP Journal on Wireless Communications and Networking (2012)

22. Cacciapuoti, A.S., Calcagno, C., Caleffi, M., Paura, L.: CAODV: Routing in Mobile Ad-hoc Cognitive Radio Networks. In: Proc. of IEEE IFIP Wireless Days 2010, Venice, Italy, October 20-22 (2010)

23. Cacciapuoti, A.S., Akyildiz, I.F., Paura, L.: Optimal Primary-User Mobility Aware Spectrum Sensing Design for Cognitive Radio Networks. To Appear in IEEE Journal on Selected Areas in Communications (JSAC)-Cognitive Radio Series (2013)

Attack Potential and Efficient Security Enhancement of Automotive Bus Networks Using Short MACs with Rapid Key Change

Sebastian Bittl

Fraunhofer ESK, 80686 Munich, Germany
sebastian.bittl@esk.fraunhofer.de

Abstract. A number of successful attacks on automotive bus systems has been published recently. However, only a limited amount of detailed studies about attack surfaces as well as efficient security mechanisms have been proposed. Therefore, a general study of possible attacks regarding content manipulation on popular automotive bus systems is provided in this work. Additionally, a new authentication scheme for bus messages is proposed, which overcomes some of the limitations imposed by previously suggested technologies. Thereby, a combination of the upcoming SHA-3 standard with standard HMAC authentication is used to achieve a highly secure system, while keeping the introduced overhead very low.

Keywords: automotive buses, Keccak, IIMAC, security.

1 Introduction

During the last years a number of serious advances regarding attacks on automotive bus systems has been proposed. Thereby, practical attacks are described in detail in [14, 16]. Furthermore, a theoretical study is provided in [20].

An introduction to the real time forensics of modern automotive bus systems is given in [7]. Together with the work provided in references [14, 16], this shows clearly that pure security by obscurity, i.e., keeping encoding of the bus contents secret, is not able to hold any serious attacker back.

Additionally, in the wake of upcoming deployment of wireless Car-to-X communication systems, like ETSI ITS in Europe [1], also in-vehicle security gains increased attention. One important reason for this is that these systems are intended to be used for safety critical applications, even during so called Day 1 use cases from 2015 on. Therefore, the Car-to-Car Communication Consortium's Working Group Security is currently on its way to define a hierarchy of trust levels for information broadcasted by vehicles. Thereby, high trust levels are very likely to require secure in-vehicle communication [17].

Recent work in the area of in-vehicle security, especially focusing on the Controller Area Network (CAN) bus, can be found in [13, 22–25]. Thereby, security enhancements are provided by applying asymmetric cryptography for authentication and key distribution among in-car controllers. The latter is used in combination with full encryption of all bus messages in reference [25]. In contrary,

A. Sikora et al. (Eds.): Nets4Cars/Nets4Trains/Nets4Aircraft 2014, LNCS 8435, pp. 113–125, 2014.

work in [22–24] uses a keyed-hash message authentication code (HMAC) [8, 15] for message authentication, which is placed as part of the message's payload. These systems use a central controller, called super gateway in [25]. It authenticates the other controllers in the car as well as generates and distributes session keys to them.

The approach described in the following differs quite significantly from the work mentioned above. Thereby, the developed approach aims to provide a generic mechanism to secure bus access on all of the commonly used automotive buses. Thereby, CAN [3], FlexRay [4], LIN [5] and MOST [18] buses are taken into regard. In order to achieve that goal, we make use of the already existing data fields for error detection. These are present in all modern automotive bus systems. Such data fields are typically filled with CRCs [3–5, 18]. These kind of checksums are only designed for pure error detection required by a noisy transmission channel. However, they do not offer any cryptographically reasonable security. Hence, we propose to exchange the contents of these fields with modern message authentication codes (MACs) like, e.g., HMACs [8, 15].

In doing so, any changes on the overall protocol structure or the size of data fields are avoided in order to keep the effort of shifting already used systems to our new design as small as possible. Especially, the design does not change the messages' payload field, thereby keeping the required bandwidth on the bus constant. This also means that processing of the MACs can be easily done independently from processing the payload, i.e., existing high level applications can be kept without modifications. Additionally, no modification of the physical layer is required by the proposed design. Such a combination of features cannot be achieved with any of the reference systems from [13, 22–25].

The remaining part of this work is outlined as follows. First of all, Section 2 gives an overview about related work in the area of attacks on automotive bus security. Moreover, the introduced concepts get generalised to the larger set of bus technologies looked at in this work. Afterwards, Section 3 studies the impact of attacks as well as data fields usable for countermeasures. Section 4 proposes a system for generating the required MACs for bus messages. Finally, a conclusion about the achieved results is presented in Section 5.

2   Related Work and Attack Surfaces of Bus Systems

The harmfulness of attacks on certain automotive bus systems is roughly categorised in [25]. Therein, further analysis mostly deals with the possibility to perform denial-of-service like attacks. Such attacks can be clearly used to prevent certain controllers from executing their regular duties. An example therefore is given in [24]. However, it is typically impossible to force a controller to execute dedicated complex tasks by just stripping it from accessing the bus. Therefore, higher level attacks, like the ones shown in [14, 16], use detailed manipulation and insertion of dedicated messages on automotive bus systems.

In the work published in [24], insertion of additional authentication bits into a CAN message frame with the so called CAN+ mechanism is studied. Unfortunately, this mechanism requires changes to the bus access hardware (physical layer). Furthermore, this approach is not generically portable to the other bus systems studied in this work. Therefore, this scheme is only used as a reference for achievable security on a CAN bus in the following.

Moreover, reference [13] focuses on bus technologies differing from ones regarded in this work, like, e.g., extensions of the standard CAN bus. Hence, the proposed approach is not looked at in detail in the following.

A very important type of attack which can be used to achieve the above mentioned data manipulation is a man-in-the-middle type of attack. Therefore, it is studied in the following Section 2.1. Afterwards, Section 2.2 studies in detail how fast an attacker can perform an attack utilising a certain bus technology.

2.1   Man-In-The-Middle Attacks

An attacker, who is assumed to have full physical access to the car and its bus systems, can perform a man-in-the-middle attack [21] as illustrated in Figure 1.

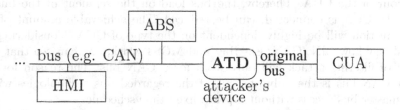

Fig. 1. A man-in-the-middle attack on an automotive bus system

Figure 1 shows the case of just one controller (called controller under attack (CUA)) being on one side of the shown single attack device (called ATD). The other controllers are just given for illustration purposes. Clearly, the attacker can also place the device in a way to separate the bus at an arbitrary point, e.g., separating one half of the controllers from the other one. Additionally, the pure bus architecture allows for an arbitrary amount of controllers to be placed in the network. For full control over the network it should always be sufficient to place one ATD in front of every controller, except of an arbitrarily chosen one. The only negative influence, an attacker has to be aware of, is additional delay caused by the ATDs.

For LIN and CAN the delay caused by the ATD should be small as direct forwarding of received data is possible. One just has to read one full symbol on the bus in order to modify and forward it, causing at least one symbol delay for the attacker. Additionally, it is possible to use available industry standard development or testing hardware for this purpose, e.g., CANLog4 from GiN [2]. On a FlexRay or MOST bus the delay is given by $dt = n * cycletime$ (with n being a positive integer), due to the used time division multiple access (TDMA) scheme. Like for CAN, ready to use hardware is available for performing such an attack for FlexRay, e.g., n = 1 holds for TTX-Connextion from TTTech [6].

Whether the functionality of a controller is limited by the caused delay is highly application specific. However, one can assume that for CAN buses, due to the small caused delay together with the CAN characteristic of being a random access bus (which must be tolerated by the application) no limiting in the available functionality has to be expected. This might be different for controllers using a FlexRay connection. This type of connection is typically used for time critical communication. Therefore, quite small and strictly monitored timeout intervals have to be assumed for this kind of applications.

2.2   Attack Speed

In [23], the authors assume that the bus load on a certain bus ([23] takes only CAN buses into regard) is a limiting factor for attacking a controller. Unfortunately, this is only partly true, even for a CAN bus, as outlined in the following.

Using a man-in-the-middle attack, the attacker can filter out all the messages on the bus which are not received by or are not necessary for the intended behaviour of the CUA. Thereby, the bus load on the segment of the bus, to which the CUA is connected, can be reduced. The achievable amount of bus load reduction will be highly dependent on the type of CUA. Considering the general way how LIN, CAN, FlexRay and MOST work, one can see that such a kind of filtering attack will only work for a CAN bus. The reason for this is that CAN bus is the only one out of the regarded bus technologies with a multi-master bus access without a-priori fixed time schedule.

In contrary, on a LIN bus, slaves are only allowed to send data after having received a corresponding pull request from the LIN master. Messages sent to the master without a preceding pull command will be simply dropped. This means the available bandwidth for attacking a LIN master, by an ATD replacing a dedicated LIN client, is defined by the corresponding pull frequency and cannot be increased by the ATD. However, this can be done for attacking LIN slaves by an ATD replacing the LIN master. Therefore, this ATD has to send additional pull commands to the CUA. In a man-in-the-middle setup, the ATD can thereby use the full bandwidth of the LIN bus for an attack on a LIN slave.

In reference [24] limitations on the available attack speed on CAN buses are described briefly. Thereby, it is assumed that a controller sends an error frame on the bus in case validation of a received message fails. The described circumvention of a too high receive error counter (REC) can be achieved by the attacker setup described above. Generalising this idea to the other regarded bus systems shows that such a limitation only exists for the CAN and MOST bus systems. The reason for this is the differing error detection and handling for the different buses. An overview of the used schemes, applied after error detection in a received message, is given in Table 1.

Table 1. Error detection and handling on the different automotive buses

bus system	LIN	CAN	FlexRay	MOST
react. to err.	opt. error flag set cont. sending	error frame sent temp. stop sending	none cont. sending	auto retry cont. sending
std. receiver resp.	none	ACK or error frame	none	ACK / NAK

An error frame gets sent on a CAN bus after a controller rejects a received frame. However, it should still be possible for an attacker to prevent detection of his attack by other controllers on the same bus. To accomplish this, he just blocks the error frame, i.e., he does not forward it. This would be sufficient from the pure bus protocol perspective, but typically timeout detection is applied for important (or even all) cyclically sent messages by their corresponding receivers. Obviously, a controller does not transmit normal data while being in bus state error (i.e., sending or just having sent an error frame). Therefore, it is quite likely for a timeout to occur at one or multiple receivers following a failed attack.

In order to circumvent such a timeout detection, the attacker can use a store and delay scheme before executing his attack. This is possible due to the non-deterministic multi-master bus access scheme (without fixed TDMA slots). Hence, no strict timeout supervision of CAN messages can be applied. Instead, one has to relax the timeout supervision to allow more time to elapse between two sequentially sent messages than the a-priori defined cycle time. Otherwise, timeout supervision would ban the system from working properly even in case all components are working properly. Exploiting this time reserve carefully, the attacker can delay messages he receives from the CUA somewhat before forwarding them. Thereby, he can accumulate the overall delay over multiple received messages and store some of them in an internal FIFO buffer for later sending. These valid messages are sent by the attacker during the time an error frame is sent by the CUA following an attack. Thereby, other controllers will not notice the attack. As a side effect, the message receivers receive outdated data. Unfortunately, CAN messages typically do not carry time stamps. Therefore, only plausibility checks can be used by the receivers to try to detect such an attack.

On a LIN bus, an attacker executing a man-in-the-middle attack can clearly filter out a set error flag. Thereby, he can avoid that further entities listening on the bus detect that one entity detected an error. In case of MOST, automatic retry of transmission is performed on both control and packet channel [18]. The number of maximum retries is implementation specific. Therefore, the bandwidth an attacker can use for an attack between the points in time which require sending of a valid packet to avoid a fatal bus error is also implementation specific.

Furthermore, no limitation of attack bandwidth by error handling is enforced by the FlexRay bus protocol. However, the absence of an error response is not always an advantage for an attacker. Thereby, he is stripped of the possibility to use non-compromised controllers as oracles, e.g., to check whether a guessed key is correct or not. Such a mechanism is briefly outlined in [24] for CAN.

Such kind of information hiding also implies that a LIN bus not using the optional error signaling together with a secure authentication mechanism should be more robust against attacks, compared to a scheme using such kind of error signaling. We come back to this point later on.

3   Attack Potential and Data Fields for Security

In reference [25] the possible impacts of attacks on the different bus systems are categorised. Thereby, it was found that attacks on CAN and FlexRay pose bigger risks than attacks on the other regarded bus systems. However, work conducted in [14] showed that all available communication interfaces may be used by an attacker to compromise controllers in an automotive network. As wireless communication interfaces are beyond the scope of this work, we concentrate on securing wired communication in the following.

Table 2 gives an overview about available CRC data fields within existing automotive bus system standards. Additionally, the impact potentials of an attack on the different bus systems are given along the lines outlined in [25].

Table 2. Length of CRC fields on different automotive bus systems

bus type	LIN	CAN	FlexRay	MOST
size of CRC field (bits)	8	15	$11 + 24$	32
impact potential	low	high	very high	low

As one can see from Table 2, the size of available data fields reserved within message frames for CRCs varies quite significantly. Fortunately, for LIN, CAN and FlexRay this field size increases alongside with increasing impact potential. FlexRay uses two different CRCs. One is embedded in the message header and guards only the header content. The other one is placed in the message's trailer and is calculated over the data section of the message. However, one could give up this separation and guard the whole message using 35 bits. Furthermore, MOST control as well as packet channel offer the same and quite significant amount of 32 bits usable for securing the communication.

Available amount of bits for securing LIN bus messages is obviously very limited (see Table 2). Even in case an attacker cannot calculate the MAC, he has still the quite high probability of $p = \frac{1}{2^8} = \frac{1}{256}$ of just guessing the correct MAC (replacing the CRC). In case one does not want to change the frame structure to provide more bits for security, other mechanisms like plausibility checks over multiple, sequential frames have to be applied for increasing the security level. As the probability of guessing correctly n times in a row decreases with p^n, a value of about three to four for n should be sufficient for most applications.

The system from [24] achieves 15 bit security via the additional bits transmitted by the CAN+ mechanism. This is identical to the level of security provided by replacing the standard CAN bus CRC with a secure MAC (see Table 2).

4 Security Enhancement by Short MACs

In the following sections the newly designed security system for bus messages is described and compared to existing solutions in detail.

4.1 Applying MACs to Bus Messages

As mentioned above, the bus messages' CRC data fields are used for storing the MACs in our design. Thereby, each controller inside the network uses its own secret key to authenticate its transmit messages. It is important that this key is reasonable long, e.g., with a length of 256 bits. Methods for obtaining the key for a dedicated message are described later on.

Quite a number of different mechanisms exist for calculating MACs. These include HMAC [8, 15] (used in [24]), CMAC [11] and GMAC [12]. Unfortunately, the use of GMAC (which has high computational performance [21]) is problematic in connection with short length MACs [12]. Therefore, it is not taken into regard in the following (see also Table 2).

The other two mentioned MAC schemes can provide a comparable level of security when the corresponding parameters are chosen carefully. Therefore, selection of the scheme to be used can be done based on its computational performance. This is a quite significant property, as the studied bus systems are usually used by embedded systems with limited available computing power. Hence, HMAC with Keccak as underlying hash function is chosen for our security mechanism, as it can be implemented in very fast way (which should clearly outperform CMAC on most systems) [9, 10, 21].

An important preliminary for avoiding a vulnerability to replay attacks is the ability to distinguish different messages. In an automotive bus system, typically many controllers will transmit the same content very often as their internal state stays the same. Moreover, none of the regarded bus systems uses a time stamp for its messages. Only FlexRay uses a cycle counter (with 6 bits length [4]). None of the systems from [25, 23] offers a solution to this problem. Authors of [24] suggest to embed a message counter into each message with each value only used once while the secret key stays constant. Required bit size of the counter is limited by changing the key each time the system restarts. Furthermore, in [13] a bit size of about 20 bits is suggested for a CAN bus when the key gets changed every hour. Obviously, a mechanism for synchronous key switching on all participating controllers is required for performing that on the fly. Due to the centralised nature of the system the super gateway should initiate this procedure.

A simple and effective solution for the described problem is to leave the bus messages unchanged, but to frequently change the key used in computing the (H)MAC. Thereby, for each set of discriminable messages (e.g., with different sequence counter values) the same key can be used. If there is no way to discriminate the individual messages, each message has to receive its own key to calculate its MAC. As the message layout is known a-priori, the key change sequence is also fixed and known a-priori. This means that it can be done independently in each network entity, e.g., when using FlexRay, after each set of

$2^6 = 64$ messages the key gets switched using the mechanism described below. If a message counter is embedded into the payload, the upper limit of its bit size should be determined following the rules given in [8, 15] together with the MAC bit sizes from Table 2 to avoid possibilities of a birthday attack.

One possible scheme for performing the key changing task is to follow the so called HMAC based one time password (HOTP) scheme from [19]. Thereby, one would use a dedicated static master secret key s_0 for each network component of recommended bit length 256 and generated at random. The individual keys s_i (with $i > 0$ being a natural number called session key counter) are derived from s_0. To do so, one applies $HMAC(s_0|i)$, whereby | means serial concatenation and HMAC is the standard algorithm known from [8]. For a HMAC scheme to have suitable performance, one should use a fast underlying hash function. To speed up key generation even more, one can safely substitute the HMAC with a hash function without length extension vulnerability in the scheme described before. Therefore, we propose to use the Keccak hash function h_k [9, 10] (upcoming SHA-3 standard) to determine s_i from s_0 according to the following equation.

$$s_i = h_k(s_0|i)$$

Thereby, the length of s_i clearly depends on the size of the output of h_k with a maximum of 512 bits according to [9, 10]. To avoid unnecessary overhead we limit the size of s_i to 256 bits by standard truncation like recommended in [10].

It is important for the system's security to ensure that i is a strictly increasing number while s_0 stays unchanged. Otherwise, possibilities to perform replay attacks may arise. In order to calculate the required bit size for i one has to take into account the buses' bit rates as well as the time span after which an overflow in i can be tolerated. Thereby, we apply the following assumptions.

The vehicle is assumed to be operated for 8 hours a day (e.g., a taxi) and an overflow of i should not happen more frequently than each 20 years. This means that s_0 is not changed during the vehicle's expected lifetime. Additionally, the worst case assumption of a single controller using the full bandwidth of a bus is taken. This leads to a maximum in the number of messages sent by this single controller. Furthermore, it is assumed that each single message gets it own session key s_i (i.e., no sequence counters in the payload are used). Results for the required bit length of i for the different bus systems are given in Table 3. Please note, that the result for MOST is independent of the used data rate (MOST 25, MOST 50 or MOST 150) as the number of sent message frames does not change between the different versions.

The obtained values for s_i are used as the secret keys in calculating the HMAC of one or multiple messages as described above. Please note, that it is not re-

Table 3. Required bit lengths of the session sequence number i

	LIN (20 Kbit/s)	CAN (1 Mbit/s)	FlexRay (20 Mbit/s)	MOST (25/50/150 Mbit/s)
length of i in bits	36	42	41	44

quired to keep the current value of i secret [19]. Therefore, it is possible to do resynchronization between different controllers if one or multiple of them get out of step, e.g., due to an unexpected reset. This can be done by exchanging dedicated messages which contain i and are signed by corresponding s_i. Two dedicated messages, one for requesting as well as one for responding, for each controller in the network should suffice to implement such a scheme.

4.2   Safe Key Storage and High Security Modules

In order to implement a secure system with the authentication strategy outlined in Section 4.1, it is necessary to provide secure storage and handling of sensitive key material. Details about available strategies for building so called high security modules (HSMs) providing such functionality are beyond the scope of this work. Therefore, the reader is referred to [23] and references within for more information on this topic.

The suggested authentication strategy requires to permanently store just the master secrets s_0 of communicating entities in a secret and not tamperable way. As outlined above, the corresponding session counter i only needs to be protected against tampering (e.g., resetting), but does not need to be kept secret. Moreover, the session keys s_i have to be kept secret as long as they are valid. For example, all keys s_n with $n < m$ and m being the current valid value of i are invalid. As there is no need to keep used session keys, they should not be stored but deleted. Additionally, the Keccak hash function is the only cryptographic primitive which has to be implemented in the HSM following the design from Section 4.1.

References [13, 22–25] suggest a centralised key distribution scheme. Mentioned reasons for such a design include good maintainability (e.g., exchanging controllers which have failed) and the possibility to keep the key generation at a single point which is specially secured. The scheme described in Section 4.1 can be used in such a setup, with the master key s_0 being generated anew by the central super node after each system start up for every network entity. Obviously, one requires to additionally include a secure key distribution procedure like the one described in [23, 25] in such a setup. Moreover, in that case the required length of i is smaller than in Table 3, as the lifetime of s_0 is much smaller, too.

In contrary, storing fixed master keys in each controller does not require support for a key distribution scheme on the fly. Additionally, one does not introduce a single point of failure into the network, as a failure of the super node obviously leads to severe restriction of the functionality of the whole system.

Unfortunately, a centralised system does not limit the requirement of an HSM in each individual controller. Secure key storage is also required in such a system. Otherwise, an attacker could just perform a man-in-the-middle attack with session hijacking. Thereby, he just forwards the messages of the CUA until he has obtained the secret session key from it. Afterwards, he hijacks the CUA's session and uses the obtained session key to authenticate his own messages. Thereby, the message receivers have no possibility to recognise the attack.

Furthermore, the centralised systems need a secure random key generator inside the HSM of the super node. In contrary, the system suggested in Section 4.1 has no such requirement. Thereby, master keys can be generated at production time of the components. Afterwards, there is no need to change these keys during active usage of the systems.

4.3   Important Properties of the Security Scheme

After its introduction in Section 4.1, the suggested algorithm is analysed in detail and gets compared to other proposed schemes in the following subsections. At first, computational performance is taken into regard. Afterwards, a close look on required bandwidth for communication is taken. Finally, the basic security features of regarded schemes are compared.

Computational Performance. No experimental data regarding computational performance is given in references [22, 23, 25]. In general, the CRCs of automotive bus systems are calculated by support of dedicated hardware. Such kind of hardware is typically included in the respective bus controllers. This is also possible for the cryptographic primitives suggested for usage in Section 4.1, as outlined in [21]. Thereby, HMAC (with Keccak) has been chosen as the CRCs' replacement due to its high performance. Therefore, the required computational performance should not limit the usability of the approach from Section 4.1.

Communication Bandwidth. The scheme from Section 4.1 does not require any changes to be made in the payload of bus messages. Therefore, the bandwidth required to transmit a certain amount of data using the bus is not changed by applying the scheme. However, the introduction of additional control messages containing the session key counter can increase the required bandwidth on the bus. As outlined in Section 4.1, the frequency of sending this kind of messages should be very low in reasonable implementations. Therefore, the influence of the security system on the required communication bandwidth of the individual controllers can be expected to be very low to negligible.

The system from references [22, 23] adds an additional overhead of 32 bits per (CAN) message to the required transmission bandwidth. As the maximum payload size of a CAN message is 64 bits, this leads to an overhead of at least 50% regarding bandwidth on the bus. In case of messages shorter than 32 bits, the relative overhead is even higher.

Moreover, the CANAuth technology [24] requires to include an additional sequence counter into each message. Thereby, required bit size of the counter is about 23 bits (taking the number of 20 bits for a counter lasting one hour from [13] and assuming the counter should not have an overflow before 8 hours). In case of porting this approach to other bus systems with higher bandwidth like MOST, one would require a much longer bit field for the message counter. Thereby, higher level applications typically do not require such a long message counter. Therefore, the counter has to be regarded as an additional data field required by security requirements,i.e., as overhead. In case of a CAN bus, the relative overhead is given by $\frac{23}{64} \approx 0.36 = 36\%$. This is clearly lower than the above mentioned overhead of systems from [22, 23]. However, it is still quite significant and may therefore limit the usability of the system.

Authors of reference [25] do not make a comment on suitable encryption algorithms. In case a block cipher (like the well known AES [21]) gets used for encrypting the messages, the possibility of using variable length messages given in the LIN and CAN protocols is stripped down. Only multiples of the cipher block size can be used when applying such an encryption scheme. Therefore, one can assume that the required communication bandwidth is at least as high as for the non-encrypted system. Thereby, equality only holds in case all messages in the standard system use a message size being a multiple of the cipher block size. In all other cases the required bandwidth is increased by using the system from [25].

Security. The security of reference systems from [22, 23] decreases significantly over time, as already outlined in [22, 23]. This is caused by the static session key which cannot be changed without restarting the whole system (e.g., vehicle). Thereby, with growing number of messages secured by the same key in combination with a quite short length MAC the probability of a successful birthday attack increases over time.

In contrary, the approach from Section 4.1 is not affected by this weakness due to the used key changing scheme. Thereby, the provided security level can be kept constant independently of the runtime of the system.

As the system from reference [25] does not use MACs at all, its resistance to eroding security over time is governed by different properties. Thereby, it is important that collecting cipher texts encrypted by the same key does not significantly help the attacker to either obtain the key or the plain messages. For reasonable encryption schemes (well chosen combination of algorithm and key length) this should not be an issue.

5   Conclusion

Securing in-vehicle communication between different embedded controllers gains more and more importance. The reasons being the publishing of more advanced attacks and a need for security in C2X applications involving data sources from multiple vehicles.

The attack potential of man-in-the-middle attacks on different common automotive bus systems was studied in detail. Thereby, it was found that random access technologies like CAN can be attacked more easily than systems using strict TDMA schemes like FlexRay.

A new approach to achieve secure in-vehicle data exchange has been proposed. In contrary to preceding work, the suggested approach does not increase the required bandwidth for communication on the target bus technology. Additionally, the algorithm can be used for all of the common bus technologies CAN, FlexRay,

LIN and MOST and can be expected to be easily portable to similar technologies as well. Moreover, the proposed scheme offers a constant security level during all its runtime and keeps its overhead at a minimum level. Therefore, it can be regarded as well usable for securing future in-vehicle communication.

References

1. Memorandum of Understanding for OEMs within the CAR 2 CAR Communication Consortium on Deployment Strategy for cooperative ITS in Europe, v 4.0102 (June 2011)
2. CANlog4. giN - Gesellschaft für industrielle Netzwerke (December 2013), http://gin.de/index.php?device=1004&lang=en
3. ISO 11898-1:2003 Road vehicles – Controller area network (CAN) – Part 1: Data link layer and physical signalling (February 2013)
4. ISO 17458-2:2013 Road vehicles – FlexRay communications system – Part 2: Data link layer specification (January 2013)
5. ISO/DIS 17987-3 Road vehicles – Local Interconnect Network (LIN) – Part 3: Protocol specification (November 2013)
6. TTX-Connexion. TTTech (December 2013), http://www.tttech.com/products/automotive/testing-tools/signal-routing/ttx-connexion/
7. Al-Kuwari, S., Wolthusen, D.: On the Feasibility of Carrying Out Live Real-Time Forensics for Modern Intelligent Vehicles. In: Forensics in Telecommunications, Information and Multimedia: Third International ICST Conf., pp. 207–223 (2010)
8. Bellare, M., Canetti, R., Krawczyk, H.: Keying Hash Functions for Message Authentication. In: Koblitz, N. (ed.) CRYPTO 1996. LNCS, vol. 1109, pp. 1–15. Springer, Heidelberg (1996)
9. Bertoni, G., Daemen, J., Peeters, M., Van Assche, G.: The Keccak sponge function family (June 2013), http://keccak.noekeon.org/
10. Chang, S., Perlner, R., Burr, W.E., Turan, M.S., Kelsey, J.M., Paul, S., Bassham, L.E.: Third Round Report of the SHA-3 Cryptographic Hash Algorithm Competition. Tech. rep., NIST (November 2012)
11. Dworkin, M.: Recommendation for Block Cipher Modes of Operation: The CMAC Mode for Authentication. NIST Special Publication 800-38B, NIST (May 2005)
12. Dworkin, M.: Recommendation for Block Cipher Modes of Operation: Galois/Counter Mode (GCM) and GMAC. NIST Special Publication 800-38D, NIST (November 2007)
13. Groza, B., Murvay, S., van Herrewege, A., Verbauwhede, I.: LiBrA-CAN: A Lightweight Broadcast Authentication Protocol for Controller Area Networks. In: Pieprzyk, J., Sadeghi, A.-R., Manulis, M. (eds.) CANS 2012. LNCS, vol. 7712, pp. 185–200. Springer, Heidelberg (2012)
14. Koscher, K., et al.: Experimental Security Analysis of a Modern Automobile. In: 31st IEEE Symposium on Security and Privacy, vol. 31 (2010)
15. Krawczyk, H., Bellare, M., Canetti, R.: HMAC: Keyed-Hashing for Message Authentication. Tech. Rep. RFC2104, Network Working Group, IETF (February 1997)
16. Miller, C., Valasek, C.: Adventures in Automotive Networks and Control Units (2013), http://illmatics.com/car_hacking.pdf
17. Moser, M.: Trust Evaluation and Trust Assurance, Protection Profiles, 7th CAR 2 CAR Forum (November 2013)

18. MOST Cooperation: MOST Specification (July 2010)
19. M'Raihi, D., Bellare, M., Naccache, D., Ranen, O.: HOTP: An HMAC-Based One-Time Password Algorithm. Tech. Rep. RFC: 4226, Network Working Group, IETF (December 2005)
20. Nisch, P.: Security Issues in Modern Automotive Systems (June 2012),
http://www.panisch.com/wp-content/uploads/2012/06/
Security_Issues_in_Modern_Automotive_Cars.pdf
21. Paar, C., Pelzl, J.: Understanding Cryptography, 2nd edn. Springer (2010)
22. Schweppe, H., Roudier, Y.: Security Issues in Vehicular Systems: Threats, Emerging Solutions and Standards. In: 5th Conference on Network Architectures and Information Systems Security (May 2010)
23. Schweppe, H., Roudier, Y., Weyl, B., Apvrille, L.: Car2X Communication: Securing the Last Meter - A Cost-Effective Approach for Ensuring Trust in Car2X Applications Using In-Vehicle Symmetric Cryptography. In: 2011 IEEE Vehicular Technology Conference (VTC Fall), pp. 1–5 (September 2011)
24. Van Herrewege, A., Singelee, D., Verbauwhede, I.: CANAuth - A Simple, Backward Compatible Broadcast Authentication Protocol for CAN bus. In: ECRYPT Workshop on Lightweight Cryptography 2011 (January 2011)
25. Wolf, M., Weimerskirch, A., Paar, C.: Security in Automotive Bus Systems. In: Proceedings of the Workshop on Embedded Security in Cars (escar) 2004 (2004)

Optimization for Wireless Vehicular Network System in Urban Area

Tsutomu Tsuboi[1] and Tatsuya Sekiguchi[2]

[1] Hamamatsu Agency for Innovation
3-5-1, Johoku Naka-ku,Hamamatsu, Shizuoka 432-8561, Japan
tsuboi@haipro.jp
[2] The University of Tokyo
7-3-1 Hongo, Bunkyo-ku, Tokyo 113-8656, Japan
ta-sekiguchi@ua.t.u-tokyo.ac.jp

Abstract. This paper aims to optimize the usefulness of the next generation vehicular network system so call WAVE (Wireless Access in Vehicle Environment) especially in urban areas that have heavy traffic density and high potential traffic accidents. The wireless vehicular technology is mainly based on DSRC (Dedicated Short Range Communication) technology defined by IEEE (Institute of Electrical and Electronics Engineers Inc.) and ETSI (European Telecommunication Standard Institute). The WAVE system is going to be used for safety and comport of vehicle mobility, for example, to avoid collision of car to car, car to other mobility and car to pedestrian and to reduce traffic congestion. In order to achieve those purposes, WAVE system is installed in vehicles as OBU (On Board Unit) and set at road side as RSU (Road Side Unit). Therefore, it is important how to set RSUs appropriate position. Authors analyze traffic condition and traffic accident condition of typical urban metropolitan area such as Tokyo and provide RSU setting guide from urban development point of view.

Keywords: DSRC, WAVE, IEEE802.11p, ITS, wireless vehicular network.

1   Introduction

The WAVE system is designed for ITS (Intelligent Transport System) which supports safety technology for automotive application. The next generation WAVE and or DSRC technology has being evaluated since 2007 when European Telecommunication Standard Institute has started TC-ITS (Technical Committee – Intelligent Transport System) group. There are several field trials especially European automotive committee such as Car to Car Communication Consortium (C2C-CC). There are also same activities in North America such as "IntelliDrive [SM]" [1] project under MOT (Ministry Of Transportation). In Asia especially in Japan, ETC (Electric Toll Correction) system has been well established since 1997 and try to expand this technology to ITS. The ETC market in Japan is 4.3 million units in 2011[2]. The ETC technology uses 5.8GHz frequency band. After 2010 when analog terrestrial services has been terminated, UHF (Ultra High Frequency) band especially 700MHz band has been open from 2011. Japanese MIC (Ministry of Internal Affairs and

A. Sikora et al. (Eds.): Nets4Cars/Nets4Trains/Nets4Aircraft 2014, LNCS 8435, pp. 126–142, 2014.
© Springer International Publishing Switzerland 2014

Communications) has assigned 9MHz bandwidth in 700MHz band for ITS, not only 5.8GHz band. In this paper, authors analyze existing metropolitan traffic conditions and accident conditions, and then provide appropriate RSU setting guidance in order to reduce traffic jams and traffic accidents efficiently. In this paper, RSU is defined WAVE base station of wireless vehicle network and it is used as vehicle to Infrastructure networks (V2I) application.

In Section 2, it describes analysis of metropolitan traffic accident statistics, provides relation between WAVE RSU setting allocation and WAVE system coverage. In section 3, it describes WAVE system setting plan and analysis of its coverage of the central part of Tokyo. In section 4, it describes WAVE system technology specification and technology advantage which covers issues in previous section which is low WAVE system coverage area. In section 5, it summarizes wireless vehicular communication optimization setting in urban area as guidance.

It is the first time to introduce WAVE system allocation in urban area by geographical methods i.e. GIS (Geographic Information System) in this paper.

2   Metropolitan Traffic Condition Analysis

2.1   Traffic Accident in Japan

According to the world statistics for traffic accident (year 2006, 2009)[3] from MIC (Ministry of Internal Affairs and Communications), Japan is 29th rank of fatal accident number per 100 thousand population. On the other hand, the rank of vehicular accident number per 100 million vehicle and kilo meter unit is number 5th. Therefore Japanese traffic accident level caused by cars is crucial.

Here is typical traffics accident statistics [4, 5] in Japan shown in Table 1 which shows top 10 prefectures' condition. According to Table 1, Aichi, Osaka and Tokyo are most careful area in Japan.

Table 1. Metropolitan traffic condition

Prefecture	Total	Fatal	Injured	Population	unified Total	unified Fatal	unified Indured
Aichi	49,651	235	61,576	7,427	669	3.16	829
Osaka	48,212	182	57,804	8,856	544	2.06	653
Tokyo	47,429	183	54,837	13,230	358	1.38	414
Fukuoka	43,178	161	56,670	5,085	849	3.17	1114
Kanagawa	37,049	179	44,135	9,067	409	1.97	487
Shizuoka	36,946	155	48,178	3,735	989	4.15	1290
Saitama	35,600	200	43,519	7,212	494	2.77	603
Hyogo	34,056	179	42,073	5,571	611	3.21	755
Chiba	22,931	175	28,558	6,195	370	2.82	461
Gunma	18,430	106	23,306	1,992	925	5.32	1170

Note: Unified data is based on 100 pollution.

2.2   Traffic Accident Tendency in Japan

Figure 1 shows the data[3] of traffic accidents classified by the transportation ways victims use. The result is shown in Fugure 1. The total number of traffic accidents is decreasing. However there are two major accident cases according to figure 1. They are accidents under vehicle driving and vehcile to pedestrian accidents during walking.

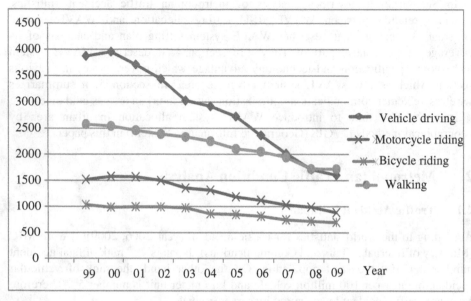

Fig. 1. Fatal accident case statistics

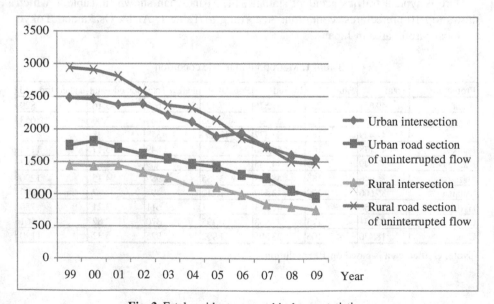

Fig. 2. Fatal accident geographical type statistics

Figure 2 shows statistics about where fatal accidents are happened. Accidents are mainly happened at intersection in urban area, and at road section of uninterrupted flow in rural area. It is celar reason for each locations for traffic accidents. There is much traffic and pedestrians at intersection in urban and it is most likely crowede area in urban. There are mis-driving in rural area such as over speed limit driving.

2.3 Tokyo Metropolitan Traffic Condition Parameters

Accdoring to section 2.1, authors choose the Tokyo area for case study as most popultaed city in Japan. The Table 2 shows Tokyo traffic density calculation process based on road traffic census data. According to the Table 2, traffic density of Tokyo becomes 115 vehicle / km^2.

Table 2. Tokyo Traffic Density (Year 2010)

	Unit	Source (formula)	Ave. Japan	Tokyo	Note
a)Ave. traffic no.	No./24h	[6]	22482	33710	
b) Day ave. traffic no.	No./12h	[6]	16331	22442	
c)Day traffic Ratio	%	b) / a)	72.6	66.5	
d) Ave, velocity	Km / h	[6]	37.7	18.7	Velocity at congested
e)Year moving distance	km	[7]	9807	8336	
f) Day moving distance	Km / day	e) / 365	26.8	22.8	24 hours
g) Day use hour	h	f) x c) / d)	0.52	0.66	day time 12 hors
h) Vehicle use ratio	%	g) / 12 hour	4.33	5.50	
i) Vehicle density	No./km2	[8] / [9]	209	2095	
j)Traffic density	No./km2	h) x i)	9.1	115	

In Table 2, authors analyse Tokyo traffic conditon based on road traffic census from MLIT (Ministry of Land, Infrastructure and Transport) year 2010[10,11]. From this result of analysis, denisty of Tokyo 23 wards is caluculated by propotion to population as in Table 3.

According to Table 3, the estimated traffic density of Tokyo 23 wards becomes 303 vehicle / km^2.

Table 3. Estimated traffic density of Tokyo 23 wards

	Area square	Population	Density	Density Ratio	Traffic density by ratio
	km2	man	Man / km2		No. / km2
Tokyo	2103	12,686,067	6,032	1.000	115
Tokyo 23 wards	538	8,575,228	15,939	2.642	303
Central 3 wards	42.16	215,433	5,109	0.846	97

2.4   Spatial Distribution of Traffic Density in Tokyo

In previous section, authors show high traffic density of Tokyo 23 wards from the data analysis. And in this section, authors make more detail a traffic condition analysis of these areas spatially. By using person trip information[12] authors show the trafic density of Tokyo 23 wards person trip. It si shown in Figure 3. Accodring to Figue 3, Tokyo central 3 wards (Chuo-ku, Chiyoda-ku and Minato-ku) have high value.

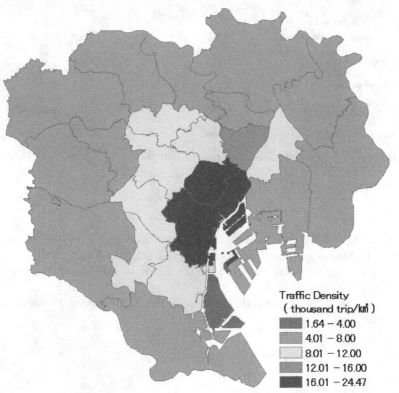

Traffic Density
(thousand trip/km)
1.64 – 4.00
4.01 – 8.00
8.01 – 12.00
12.01 – 16.00
16.01 – 24.47

Fig. 3. Tokyo traffic condtion based on person trip

From the figure3, traffic desnity becomes higher towards the center of Tokyo. The main reason of this is that the density of road network in central Tokyo is also higher than other areas. Generally speaking, there are more traffic accidents in the areas that have many roads. Therefore high traffic dcsity analysis is important for the effectiveness of WAVE RSU setting.

2.5   Tokyo 23 Wards RSU Setting and Coverage Analysis

In this section, authors analyze RSUs setting and coverage of Tokyo 23 wards based on the result of previous sections.

Authors choose cross section points of major roads in Tokyo 23 wards as the first WAVE RSU setting location because there are major accidental areas at urban intersections from Figure 2. In Figure 4, it shows the location of major intersections with WAVE RSUs setting. The target location for RSUs setting is intersections along with major roads such as national and Tokyo public roads because there are more pedestrians and vehicles than other narrower roads. The buffer from each RSU means WAVE system wireless communication range which is used experienced 274 meters from ITS Forum RC-007 document[13]. In this paper, WAVE system is used Japanese 700MHz frequency which is defined ARIB (Association of Radio Industries and Businesses) STD-T109.

Fig. 4. WAVE RSU setting in Tokyo 23 wards [14]

In terms of WAVE RSU coverage, authors use geographical coverage as the ratio of roads that are covered by the buferrs from RSUs.The calculated ratio is based on the length of each road, and result is aggragated by each area. So the caluculation formula of RSU geographical coverage is as follows;

[RSU buffer geographical coverage] =

[Road length which covered by RSU in each area] / [Total road length in each area] ----- (1)

The coverage condition in Tokyo 23 wards shows in Figure 5.

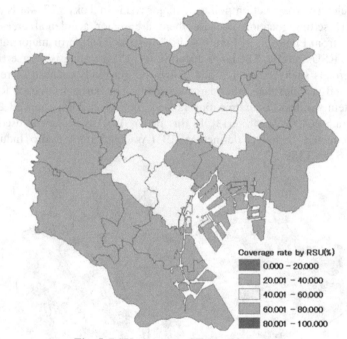

Coverage rate by RSU(%)

■ 0.000 – 20.000
■ 20.001 – 40.000
□ 40.001 – 60.000
■ 60.001 – 80.000
■ 80.001 – 100.000

Fig. 5. RSU coverage of Tokyo 23 wards

According to Figure 5, central areas of Tokyo are well covered by RSU and the coverage rate of other areas is lower than that of central areas. However it is reasonable RSU setting compared by traffic condition in Figure 3 and coverage condition in Figure 5.

3   Detail Metropolitan Case Study

According to section 2, Tokyo central three wards have many traffic accidents because of their high traffic density. Authors also show effectiveness of WAVE RSUs by setting major intersection of roads.

However the detail of roads network of each area is different. So there may be deviation of RSU coverage rate and it may not be enough for some regions to set RSU at the major intersections, if focus on the each area on fineer scall. So we have to consider additional countermeasures in such regions.

In this section, authors focus on the road network in Tokyo central 3 wards area(i.e. Chiyoda-ku, Chuo-ku and Minato-ku) whose traffic density are higher than other areas of Tokyo.The aim of this section is to take more detail about WAVE RSU setting plan.

3.1   WAVE System Setting Plan

The Figure 6 shows RSU setting in Tokyo central 3 wards.

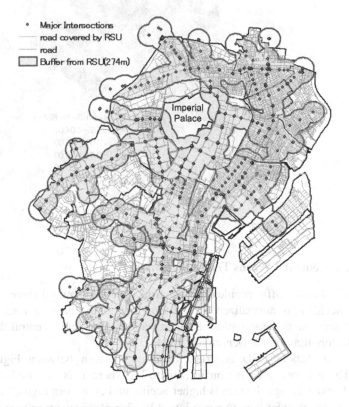

Fig. 6. WAVE RSU setting plan in Tokyo central 3 wards

In terms of WAVE RSU system coverage, it is used as same as calculation formula (1) in section 2.4.

The Figure 7 shows the WAVE RSU coverage of Tokyo central 3 wards.

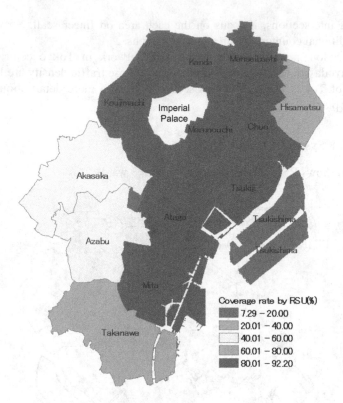

Fig. 7. WAVE RSU geographical coverage

3.2   Tokyo Central 3 Wards Traffic Accident

The Figure 8 shows traffic accident distribution of Tokyo central three wards. The number of accident is normalized by the total length of roads in each area. The data[15] authors use is the statistics of traffic accidents in Tokyo central three wards from the Metropolitan Police Department 2011.

Here is issue about RSU coverage from comparison between Figure 7 and Figure 8. There is one area Azabu in Minato-ku where it is not well covered by WAVE RSU even though the area is higher accitdental area from Figure 8. Therefore it is necessary to consider how to cover lower WAVE RSU coverage area where it is higher potential traffic accident area. This geographical limitation is caused by urban road systems i.e. the distribution of roads, intersections, traffic signals etc. Authors provide countermeassures for this issues in the next section.

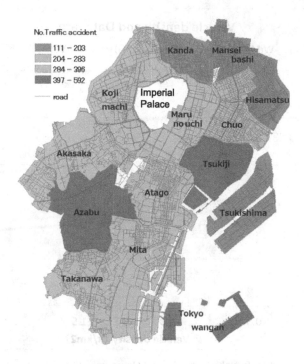

Fig. 8. Traffic accident distribution in Tokyo central three wards

4   Proper WAVE Selection under Low RSU Coverage Area

4.1   Vehicle Communication Comparison

There are several wireless communication technology such as 3GPP of cellular network, high speed data network like LTE (Long term Evolution) and or WiMAX (Worldwide Interoperability for Microwave Access). Tsuboi has studied vehicle related wireless communication network comparison among 3GPP cellular network, WiMAX and WAVE. The results were as follows[16];

- WAVE technology (700MHz and 5.9GHz) has covered high data rate communication above 10Mbps in case of less than 1,000 vehicle per 1km^2 , which is actual traffic condition (refer to Table 3).
  (Vehicle density and Data rate analysis is shown in Figure 9.)
- 3GPP and WiMAX have more than 1,000 vehicle communication coverage within their cells.
  (Vehicle density and Number of vehicle analysis is shown in Figure 10)

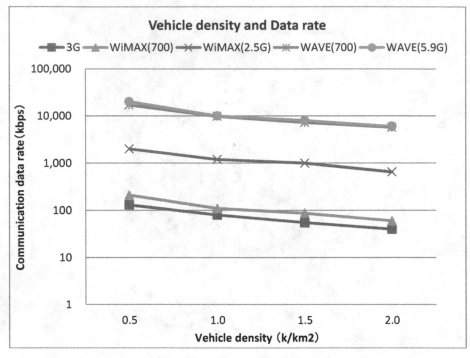

Fig. 9. Vehicle density and Communication data rate

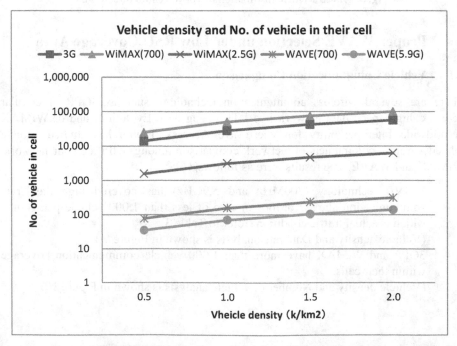

Fig. 10. Vehicle density and Number of Vehicle in cell

According to this analysis, WAVE technology has communication data rate advantage compared with 3GPP and WiMAX broadband wireless communication technology, especially it is sufficient to support multimedia application such as moving picture transmission. The moving picture is good communication tools for drivers because of drivers know real situation of traffic condition rather than just warning message. Among these wireless access technologies, the latency is key factor especially for safety application such as anti-collision. The latency of WAVE is less than 10 msec based on our measurement[17]. But the latency of 3GPP is more than 100 msec and that of LTE is around 10 msec[18].

However in terms of supporting number of vehicles in their cell, 3GPP and WiMAX have advantage than WAVE. According to Table 3 in this paper, the Tokyo 23 wards vehicle density is 303. But WAVE 700MHz system covers 80 vehicle in cell with 15Mbps data rate transmission condition. Therefore when 700MHz WAVE system covers 303 vehicles in its cell, it is necessary to calculate how much the data rate is. In WAVE system, the total data is less than 1,000 byte per packet and data is shown in Table 4 in ARIB STD-T109 specification.

Table 4. WAVE data structure

Type of data	Contents	Length（Byte）
Service	Power level, modulation type, standard	2
MAC control	MAC control, ppacket counter between OBU and R	24
Link management	Netork management information	8
Data	Feee data	Lx
FSC	Error correction	4
Pad	Data length adaptation	2
Total		40+Lx

The data rate is calculated by Table 5 under Table 4 WAVE data structure condition. In Table 5, it is used typical WAVE parameters such as bandwidth 9MHz, interval transmission 100 msec. When number of vehicle is 303, then data transmission is calculated 12.31 Mbps.

In section 4.1, WAVE technology is more sufficient for supporting multimedia data transmission such as moving picture and it also covers high density of vehicle density in metropolitan compared with other vehicle related wireless communication system.

Table 5. WAVE data rate calculation

Symbol	Contents	Unit	Value	Reference
D1	No. of Vehicle	number	303	
D2	Data	byte	508	=Lx
D3	Interval of transmission	msec	100	
D4	Transmission rate	Mbps	12.31	D1*D2/D3
D5	Effciency of frequency	bit/Hz	1.368	
D6	Bandwidth	MHz	9.00	D4/D5

4.2   WAVE Technology Comparison

Here is current WAVE technology specification comparison which is shown in Table 6. There are two types Japanese ITS standards, North America IEEE standard, and European ITS standard ETSI.   The IEEE standard is IEEE802.11p-2010/IEEE1609 and ETSI standard is ETSI ES202 663/EN102 731. IEEE and ETSI have quaterly technical meetings for harmonization each other. Therefore there is not so much differnces between them. For example, there were three channels which are one CCH and two SCHs in ETSI until 2010. But there are seven channels as total now.

Table 6. WAVE technology comparison

	Japan		USA	EU
	DSRC	700MHz	(DSRC)	(DSRC)
Application Layer	application ETC	application Anti-collision	application ●Anti-collision ●High speed data	application ●Anti-collision ●High speed data
Upper Layer Protocol	DSRC Protocol	Dedicated (current)	Application mng. IEEE1609	Application mng. UDP/TCP, IPv6 WSMP (non-IP) LLC
Access typ.	TDM/FDD	CSMA/CA	802.11p CSMA／CA	CSMA／CA
Modulation	QPSK	OFDM (BPSK/QPSK/16QAM)		
No. of channel	5MHzx7ch x2(up/down)	■CCH 9MHzx1ch	■CCH ■SCH 10MHzx7ch (20MHz option)	■CCH ■SCH 10MHzx7ch
Frequency Band	5.8GHz	700MHz	5.9GHz	5.9GHz

4.3   700MHz WAVE Technology Advantage

In section 3, there is a issue about WAVE RSU low coverage area such as Azabu in Tokyo central three wards. In terms of main traffic accidents in urban area, they are most vehcile to vehicle collision and vehcile to pedestrian in Table 1. Therefore it is important to how to cover those main traffic accidents by WAVE system not only by RSUs but also WAVE OBUs which are installed in vehicles. This WAVE OBUs are expected to perform prevent collisions by the vehcile to vehicle (V2V) commuication essentially. In this section, authors explain effectiveness about this V2V commuication system in order to support WAVE RSU low coverage area as vehcile to infrastrucrue (V2I).

The reason why authors take 700MHz WAVE rather than 5.8GHz DSRC is 700MHz WAVE communication range advantage. The range difference between 700MHz band and 5.8GHz band is around 8 time obtained by the free space propagation loss using its direct wave electic power i.e. Friss formula equation[19].

Therefore 700MHz WAVE is more capable for vehicle to vehicle communication under less RSU setting location like Azabu in this case.

In terms of wireless communication range compalison, Tsuboi[20] has analized braking distance under wet asphalt pavcment road condition by comparison among 5.8 GHz, 2.4GHz and 700MHz freaquency band WAVE/DSRC system. The Figure 11 shows the shimulation results of braking disnatnce comparison at the corner of metropolitan area which shows the image of the town in Figure 12[21]. The illustration of Figure 12 is typical metropolitan cross pont which is srounding by higher buldings. Therefore drivers who drive in those area is hard to know the condition of traffic behind the buildings.

In Figure 11, there are three different type of frequency bands of WAVE system. The line graph shows the acceptance braking disatnce for each WAVE system. The acceptance braking distance here is the distance in which one vehicle from the street driving can stop after when the vehicle receives a approaching signal from the other driving vehicle of the cross road. The bar graph shows running distance which one vehicle is able to stop when driver starts breaking vehicle. When the line graph is above the bar, it means that the vehicle can stop before the other vehicle comes into the corner of the cross point. There is no collision in this condition. On the other hand, when the line is under bar, it means there is possibility of collison between vehciles. This road condition if Figure 11 is wet asphalt pavement. According to Figure 11, it is clear that there is no potential collision under 60km per hour vehicle velocity with 700MHz WAVE system. It shows that 700MHz WAVE system has communication range advantage for NLOS (non Line of sight) communication against 2.4GHz and 5.8GHz WAVE system. This advantage becomes valid for anti-collision at low

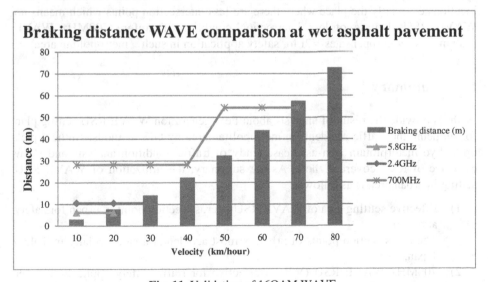

Fig. 11. Validation of 16QAM WAVE

Fig. 12. Image of typical cross point of metropolitan

coverage by RSU in urban area such as Azabu in Figure 7. According to the actual traffic accidents statistics of Azabu[14,22], there are 461 of vehicle to vehicle collision accidents in total 592 traffic accidents in 2012. And there are 125 of vehicle to pedestrian accidents, and 6 accidents of indivisual vehicle. Therefore traffic safety system has to cover traffic accidents caused by vehicle to vehicle collision in those locations especially the place where there are less intersection points which means no WAVE RSUs beuase of less intersection condition. Therefore 700MHz WAVE system of V2V compensates V2I for safety application in such   metropolitan area.

5   Summary

Authors provide the result of analysis about next generation WAVE RSU setting plan for reducing the traffic accidents in metropolitan area by GIS methods. Authors pick up Tokyo metorplotain area as a case study of traffic condition analysis and show evidence of RSU coverage there. As the summary, the utilization of WAVE RSU setting in urban area is as follows;

1) Effective settting area of WAVE RSU is cross section point in urban for safety application
   The cross section points of urban is most accidental area especially in Tokyo Japan.
2) 700MHz WAVE RSU (V2I) is effective for traffic safety application under current traffic condition in Tokyo by analysing traffic density for each area.

3) In case of low coverage area of RSUs, 700MHz frequency band WAVE system is effective by using vehicle to vehicle (V2V) communication application. 700MHz WAVE system has wireless communication range advantage compared with other WAVE system such as 5.8/5.9GHz frequency band DSRC technology.

Author take the first step for WAVE RSU setting opitimization by allocating RSU at cross points in metroplitan. And authors show that cross point section by setting of WAVE RSUs is effective for safety application especially in metoropolitan area such as Tokyo Japan. However there are also several issues of setting place for RSU in future because each location is different condition by historical develoment of towns in general. The next generation 700MHz WAVE system becomes good candidate system in future ITS application.

Acknowledgements. Authors provide appreciation to Dr.Noriaki Yoshikawa of Cyber Creative Institute for study of WAVE propagation analysis and to Prof. Noboru Hatara of The University of Tokyo and Associated Prof. Nobuaki Omori of The Uiniveristy of Tokyo for advise of traffic density and geographical analysis in Tokyo.

References

1. Ammana, A.. Overview of IntelliDrive/Vehicle Infrastructure Integration (VII) report (2009), http://filebox.vt.edu/users/aamanna/web%20page/VII-IntelliDrive%20Report-edited.pdf
2. Automobile Research Institute, http://www.jari.or.jp/resource/pdf/H22jigyo1/0711-4.pdf
3. The world statistics information of Ministry of Internal affairs and Communications, http://www.stat.go.jp/data/sekai/pdf/2009al.pdf
4. Traffic accident statistics data of National Police agency (2012), http://www.npa.go.jp/toukei/index.htm#koutsuu
5. Popultaion statistics data of MIC (Ministry of Internal Affairs and Commuications) (2012), http://www.stat.go.jp/data/nenkan/02.htm
6. Kanto area road traffic data (Road traffic census 2010), http://www.mlit.go.jp/road/census/h22-1/data/pdf/syuukei04.pdf
7. Diesel vehicle economic analysis, Gas, Hybrid comparison Mitsubishi Research Institute, http://www.meti.go.jp/committee/materials/downloadfiles/g41116b40j.pdf
8. Japan Light Motor Vehicle Inspection Organization, http://www.airia.or.jp/number/pref/2012/2012p03.pdf
9. Geospatial Information Authority of Japan, http://www.gsi.go.jp/KOKUJYOHO/MENCHO/201210/ichiran.pdf
10. Statistics Division Bureau of General Affairs, http://www.toukei.metro.tokyo.jp/juukiy/2012/jy12qf0001.pdf
11. Statistics Division Bureau of General Affairs, http://www.gsi.go.jp/KOKUJYOHO/MENCHO/201210/ichiran.pdf

12. National Land Numerical Information downloard service of MLIT (Ministry of Land, Infrastructure, Transport and Tourism),
http://nlftp.mlit.go.jp/ksj-e/index.html
13. Conthortium of ITS Promotion, ITS FORUM RC-007 document, "Technical data about the frequency sharing conditions of the driving support communications system and contiguity system using a 700MHz band" (April 2011)
14. Sumitomo Electric System Solutions co. Ltd., Digiral Road Map Database
15. Traffic accident statistics data of Metropolitan Police Department 2011 (2011),
http://www.keishicho.metro.tokyo.jp/toukei/bunsyo/toukei23/pdf/kt23d010.pdf
16. Tsuboi, T., Yamada, J., Yamauchi, N., Yoshikawa, N.: Cell design for next DSRC applications. In: ICUMT 2009, pp. 1–5 (2009)
17. Tsuboi, T.: Second International Conference on Future Generation Communication and Networking, FGCN 2008, vol. 1 (2008)
18. Rysavy reseach, LLC: mobile broadband explosion, 3GPP wireless evolution, p. 51,
http://www.4gamericas.org/documents/4G%20Americas%20Mobile%20Broadband%20Explosion%20August%2020121.pdf
19. Mobile communication council of MIC (Ministry of International Affairs and Communication) report April 2013,
http://www.soumu.go.jp/main_content/000218099.pdf
20. Friss, H.T.: A note on simple transmission formula. Proc. 34(5), 254–256 (1946)
21. Tsuboi, T.: Study of diffraction comparison among WAVE system by using single knife model. Proc. IEICE 111(441(ITS)), 147–152 (2012)
22. Hearing data from Azabu Police Station

LTE Micro-cell Deployment
for High-Density Railway Areas

Aleksander Sniady[1], Mohamed Kassab[2], José Soler[1], and Marion Berbineau[2]

[1] Networks Technology and Service Platforms, DTU Fotonik, Technical University of Denmark
DK-2800, Kgs. Lyngby, Denmark
{alesn,joss}@fotonik.dtu.dk
[2] Univ Lille Nord de France, F-59000, Lille, IFSTTAR,
LEOST, F-59650, Villeneuve d'Ascq, France
{mohamed.kassab,marion.berbineau}@ifsttar.fr

Abstract. Long Term Evolution (LTE) is a serious candidate for the future releases of the European Rail Traffic Management System (ERTMS). LTE offers more capacity and supports new communication-based applications and services for railways. Nevertheless, even with this technology, the classical macro-cell radio deployments reach overload, especially in high-density areas, such as major train stations. In this paper, an LTE micro-cell deployment is investigated in high-density railway areas. Copenhagen Main Station is considered as a realistic deployment study case, with a set of relevant railway communication-based applications. The micro-cell deployment is compared with a classical macro-cell deployment in terms of transmission performance. Simulation results show a capacity improvement in the micro-cell deployment and its positive impact on critical (safety) and non-critical applications.

Keywords: LTE, GSM-R, ETCS, ERTMS, railway signaling, mobile communication, network planning, network simulation, OPNET.

1   Introduction

The European Rail Traffic Management System (ERTMS) is a unified train control system, which has become the reference for railway management systems worldwide [1, 2]. ERTMS relies on GSM-R, as a telecommunication technology, to carry the European Train Control System (ETCS) and voice communication between ground and rolling stock.

Today, GSM-R has various shortcomings, especially limited capacity [3, 4]. Several research projects are exploring the replacement of GSM-R by the 3GPP Long Term Evolution (LTE) [5, 6]. LTE is able to support heterogeneous traffic, while ensuring Quality of Service (QoS) differentiation between various applications [7]. Taking this into account, an LTE-based telecommunication network should be able to satisfy current and future needs of railway communication systems. On the other hand, railways are increasingly demanding in terms of radio resources and real-time requirements. In fact, railway operators and infrastructure managers are asking for new communication-based applications [8], in addition to signaling and voice calls. These applications are related to security (e.g. video surveillance, and discrete

A. Sikora et al. (Eds.): Nets4Cars/Nets4Trains/Nets4Aircraft 2014, LNCS 8435, pp. 143–155, 2014.

listening), operating support (e.g. platform surveillance, remote maintenance and voice announcements) and entertainment applications (e.g. advertisment broadcasting and Internet for passengers).

Some previous studies point out that LTE may be used in railways for three types of applications [9, 10, 11]:

- Safety-critical applications (i.e. the ETCS railway signaling).
- Applications essential for railway operation (i.e. voice communication).
- Additional applications, which are not necessary for train movement (e.g. video surveillance, voice announcements, discreet listening, file update, Internet for passengers, etc.).

The mentioned studies show that these applications can coexist in a single network, without a negative impact on the performance of safety-critical applications. Moreover, the performance offered to the safety-critical and essential applications is beyond that offered by GSM-R, even in overload conditions [9, 10]. But the same results show that this improvement is limited in high-density areas [11]. This is due to the inadequacy of the macro-cell based radio coverage, which is not able to provide enough resources to all the trains when new application traffic is added. These additional applications are highly demanding in terms of bandwidth. One solution to this lack of resources could be a non-regular radio planning, adapted to the different traffic load in different railway areas.

In this paper, the interest is put on the performance that an LTE micro-cell based radio coverage can offer in high-density railway areas. This should be especially beneficial for the applications consuming a lot of bandwidth. The Copenhagen Main Station is considered as an example of a high-density area. The focus of our study is put on the communication performance (end-to-end delay and packet loss) offered to the ETCS signaling application (safety-critical), the voice call application and video surveillance application. The evolution of these performance parameters is studied in relation to the number of trains, in the considered area. The case study is modeled in a computer-based telecommunication simulator: OPNET Modeler [12].

The paper is organized as follows. Section 2 describes a set of railway applications, their requirements on communication performance and our proposed study case. Section 3 presents the simulation scenarios comparing the alternative radio deployments. Section 4 details simulation results and discussions. Finally, section 5 concludes the paper.

2   Railway Communication-Based Applications and Case Study

2.1   Railway Applications

Today, railway operators and infrastructure managers define several additional applications, along with ETCS signaling and voice communication. In our case study, a set of five typical railway applications is considered, as described below.

1. The European Train Control System (ETCS) is the signaling system defined by ERTMS. ETCS operates on a basis of data message exchanges between On-Board

Units (OBU), which are located in trains, and Radio Block Controllers (RBC), which supervise train movements. ETCS is a safety-critical application and has strict transmission performance requirements. These requirements were defined for circuit-switched based transmission over GSM-R. For packet-switched based communication, as in LTE, there are only tentative requirements available [3]. The average transfer delay of a 128-byte ETCS message is required to be lower than 500 ms. Moreover, 95% of the ETCS messages must be delivered within 1.5 s. The probability of data loss or corruption must be lower than 0.01%.

2. Interphone is the internal railway telephony, essential for railway operation. For instance, it is used for communication between a train driver and the traffic control center. In our case study, each train makes a voice call to the control center every 900 s, on average. Every interphone call generates one uplink stream and one downlink stream, both with a throughput equal to 64 kbps. The call duration is 20 s, on average. The interphone application can tolerate a maximum average delay of 150 ms and a maximum packet loss ratio of 1% [13].

3. Voice announcement informs the on-board passengers about the current traffic situation. Every train receives an announcement from the control center every 900 s, on average. Each announcement has an average duration of 5 s. The announcements generate a 64 kbps uplink stream. The voice announcement application can tolerate a maximum average delay of 150 ms and a maximum packet loss ratio of 1% [13].

4. Video surveillance continuously transmits two real-time video streams from each of the trains to the control center. Video surveillance is based on *Closed Circuit TeleVision (CCTV)* system. Every train carries two CCTV cameras. Each camera generates a constant stream of 62.5 packets (1000 bytes) every second. This application can tolerate a maximum average delay of 100 ms and a maximum packet loss ratio of 0.1%.

5. File update is an application used by the on-board equipment to upload non safety-critical information to the control center. This could be used to upload maintenance data collected by sensors in a train. The application transmits a 7 GB file in the uplink every 20 hours, on average.

2.2   Case Study

Copenhagen Main Train Station is the biggest train station in Denmark. It has a high train concentration. It is a typical area where a GSM-R network may offer insufficient capacity to serve all the trains [3].

In [10], it was established that up to 27 trains can be expected at Copenhagen Main Train Station in a peak hour. In the future, up to 40 trains are expected.

Two LTE-deployment configurations are considered for this area. Each configuration models one of the two alternative radio network deployments at Copenhagen Main Train Station.

In the first configuration, the macro-cell deployment, an LTE radio network covers the station with just a single radio cell. The cell has a radius of approximately 1 km. This configuration is illustrated in Figure 1a. In the second configuration, the micro-cell deployment, the train station is covered with a set of 10 micro-cells. Each has a radius of approximately 50 m. The micro eNodeBs are placed linearly following the linear shape of the station and the tracks to cover. This configuration setup is illustrated in Figure 1b.

In an LTE radio access network, there is interdependency between cell range, cell-edge throughput and traffic load [14]. Firstly, the smaller the cell range, the higher the cell throughput is. Hence, by deploying micro cells with much shorter range, it is expected that the cell throughput will increase. Secondly, the lower the traffic load, the higher the cell throughput is. In the micro-cell deployment, the traffic load is distributed over more cells than in the macro-cell case. Thus, the traffic load per cell is smaller and the throughput increases.

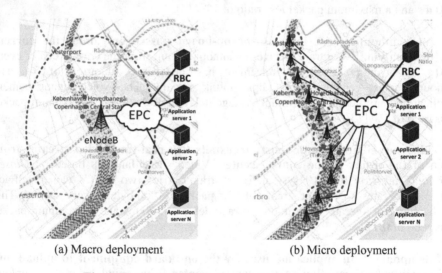

(a) Macro deployment   (b) Micro deployment

Fig. 1. The studied LTE deployments. Map source: [15].

3   LTE Deployments and QoS Configuration

3.1   Simulation Scenarios

For performance evaluation, two simulation scenarios were evaluated. Each scenario modeled one of the two LTE deployments presented in section 2.2.

The trains were modeled as LTE User Equipment (UE), which used the LTE network to connect to the application servers. LTE eNodeBs (eNBs) were connected to an Evolved Packet Core (EPC) node, which modeled the whole functionality of an LTE backbone network, i.e. the Serving Gateway (S-GW), the Packet Data Network Gateway (PDN-GW) and the Mobility Management Entity (MME). The EPC provided connectivity to the railway application servers.

The macro-cell scenario modeled an LTE radio network that covered the station with a single radio cell. The cell operated in the frequency band used currently by GSM-R. The micro-cell scenario modeled an LTE radio network that covered the station with 10 cells. Table 1 presents the parameters of both scenarios.

Our initial simulations showed that the inter-cell interference is a crucial issue in this study, but in a different manner for each scenario. In the macro-cell scenario, the inter-cell interference was modeled by four jammer nodes, deployed at the edge of the studied cell. These nodes simulated the wireless transmissions in the cells surrounding the studied LTE cell.

In the micro-cell scenario, some coordination mechanisms for inter-cell interference avoidance had to be used. For instance, eNodeBs could implement partial frequency reuse [17]. Thanks to this mechanism neighboring LTE cells do not use the same frequencies at cell edges. However, the LTE model in OPNET does not support the partial frequency reuse mechanism. Hence, some additional configuration changes were necessary, in order to make the simulations model as close as possible to real deployments. The effect of partial frequency reuse mechanism was therefore reproduced by a second frequency band of 5 MHz. Every other micro eNodeB used this second band, i.e. two direct neighbor cells operated always in different frequencies. In this way the system performance resembled a system with partial frequency reuse.

Table 1. Simulation scenario parameters

Parameter:	Macro cell scenario	Micro cell scenario
Frequency band	920 MHz (5 MHz bw.)	5.9 GHz (5 MHz bw.)
eNB Transmission power	36 dBm	1.5 dBm
eNB antenna height	50 meters	10 meters
eNB antenna gain	15 dBi	
UE antenna gain	1 dBi	
Pathloss model	UMa[1]	UMi[2]
Multipath channel model	ITU Pedestrian A[3]	

1: ITU-R M2135 Urban Macro (UMa) [16]. The simulation randomly chooses between Line-of-Sight and Non-Line-of-Sight cases
2: ITU-R M2135 Urban Micro (UMi) [16]
3: The ITU Pedestrian A multipath channel model is chosen because the trains (UEs) in the simulations are considered stationary.

3.2   Quality-of-Service (QoS) Configuration

LTE technology offers a QoS management mechanism based on the *Evolved Packet System (EPS) bearers,* which are used to carry packets with common QoS requirements [7]. Each bearer receives a specific QoS treatment in the radio access, as well as in the core network. Each bearer has a QoS Class Identifier (QCI) associated. This QCI defines a set of node specific parameters (e.g. scheduling weights, admission thresholds, packet discard timer, etc.) that determines the packet forwarding behavior [17].

A railway communication system carries a heterogeneous set of applications. Each has different requirement, as described in section 2.1. Thus, an LTE deployment for railways must use the LTE QoS mechanisms to serve the different applications.

In this work, a QoS configuration for LTE deployments was defined, based on the application requirements presented in section 2.1. Two dedicated bearers were assigned for each of the UEs: one for the ETCS application and one for both voice applications (interphone and voice announcements). The remaining traffic was carried using the best-effort bearer, established for each UE by default. Following the recommendations of Khayat, et. al. in [10], traffic from the ETCS application was carried by a Guaranteed Bit Rate (GBR) EPS bearer. This ensures that safety-critical traffic (ETCS) receives sufficient bitrate regardless of other traffic in the network. More details of the EPS bearer configuration are shown in Table 2.

Table 2. EPS bearer configuration used in the simulations

EPS bearer:	Safety-critical bearer	Medium priority bearer	Default bearer
Application(s)	ETCS	Interphone and voice announc.	Other
QoS Class Identifier (QCI)	3 (GBR)	2 (GBR)	9 (Non-GBR)
Guaranteed bitrate (uplink)	16 kbps	64 kbps	-
Guaranteed bitrate (downlink)	16 kbps	64 kbps	-
Allocation retention priority	1	5	9
Scheduling priority[1]	3	4	9
Delay budget[1]	50 ms	150 ms	300 ms
Packet error loss rate[1,2]	10^{-3}	10^{-3}	10^{-6}
1: Values of these parameters are defined in a 3GPP standard [18]. Moreover, these values are only performance targets and are not strict requirements. 2: Maximum error loss rate in a non-congested network.			

4   Simulation Results and Discussion

For the simulation study, we use the OPNET Modeler v. 17.5. OPNET Modeler is a powerful event-driven simulation tool, offering end-to-end simulation capabilities via a rich technology and protocol library. It includes a complete LTE model with all essential LTE features and network equipment.

The simulation scenarios were analyzed in 10 subcases, with an increasing number of trains (UEs) at the station. The investigated range was from 5 to 50 UEs (1 UE per train). Thus, the analysis went beyond the maximum number of trains expected at Copenhagen Main Train Station (up to 40 trains in year 2030 [10]). Every subcase was executed 15 times, with varying random seed numbers. Each simulation run lasted 20 minutes.

In the following, four sets of results are presented. The first is related to the total throughput of the network. The following three are related to each of the considered application categories (safety-critical, essential for railway operation and additional applications).

4.1   LTE Radio Throughput

Initially, the two LTE-deployment configurations, micro-cell and macro-cell, are compared in terms of the radio link throughput. Figure 2 shows the average LTE radio throughput, in the uplink and in the downlink, in relation to the number of trains at the station.

Since the video transmission application sent data in the uplink, the uplink direction carried more traffic than the downlink, as shown in Figures 2a and 2b. Thus, the uplink results are considered to highlight the difference between the two deployments.

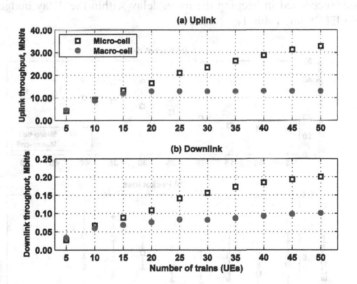

Fig. 2. Throughput in the uplink and the downlink in relation to the number of trains (UEs) at the station for the micro-cell and the macro-cell LTE deployments

In the macro-cell deployment, the average uplink throughput was increasing until the number of trains at the station reached 20. Afterwards, the throughput remained approximately constant at 12.90 Mbps, even with more trains (UEs). Here, the maximum capacity of the macro cell radio uplink was reached.

In the micro-cell deployment, the average uplink throughput increased continuously in the whole investigated range. With 50 trains at the station, the uplink throughput in the micro deployment reached 32.77 Mbps. This higher throughput, compared to the macro-cell deployment, was a result of the additional LTE cells present in the micro-cell scenario. This meant that the traffic load was spread between more cells. As a result, each of the micro-cells was utilized less than the macro-cell. Thus, the micro-cells did not reach saturation. Therefore, the micro-cell deployment offers significantly more capacity than the macro-cell deployment.

4.2   ETCS Safety-Critical Application

This subsection is focused on the communication performance experienced by the safety-critical ETCS application, when other types of traffic are simultaneously present in the network.

The first performance indicator is the mean packet transfer delay in relation to the number of trains (UEs) at the station, as shown in Figure 3a. In the macro-cell deployment, the delay increased rapidly between the subcase with 5 trains and the subcase with 20 trains. Then, the delay stabilized at, approximately, 40 ms. It should be noted, that the radio link utilization also reached saturation in the case with 20 trains. The delay did not increase further thanks to the QoS mechanism. The QoS mechanisms succeeded in keeping the mean delay within the delay budget of 50 ms targeted for ETCS (cf. Table 1).

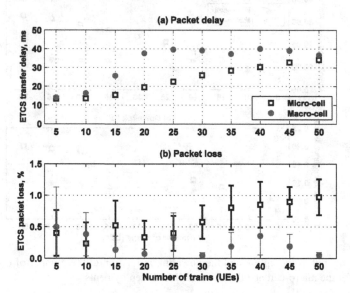

Fig. 3. Mean ETCS packet transfer delay and mean packet loss rate (with 95% confidence intervals) in relation to the number of trains

The micro-cell deployment offered a noticeably lower delay. This is because, the capacity of the micro-cells did not reach saturation. The LTE network provided transmission resources to ETCS, without the need of pre-empting other traffic. This pre-emption would increase delay. However, despite this delay performance difference, both deployments fulfilled the ETCS requirements with a large margin. The recorded values were an order of magnitude smaller than the maximum acceptable mean delay of 500 ms [3].

The second performance indicator is the packet loss rate in relation to the number of trains. According to ETCS requirements, the probability of data loss rate should not exceed 0.01% [3]. Since our ETCS model in OPNET did not include any retransmission mechanism, the data loss rate, at the application level, was equal to the packet loss at the connection level. As shown in Figure 3b, in both deployments, the packet loss rate was larger than 0.01% (between 0.04% and 1.0%).

Therefore, the packet loss rate exceeded the budget defined for this application in the QoS configuration (cf. Table 2). This is due to the inter-cell interference, which increased error rate at the radio link. This interference was higher in the micro-cell deployments. This point is discussed in more details in section 4.4.

Despite these results, which did not meet the packet loss requirements for the safety-critical application, LTE should remain a valid option for railway communication network. Indeed, ETCS tolerates packet delay up to 500 ms. Given that the measured delays are below 50 ms (cf. Fig. 3b), it is possible to retransmit a lost message, even multiple times, without reaching the delay boundary. Therefore, by implementing a retransmission mechanism, at the transport layer or at the application, the data loss rate would improve significantly and stay within ETCS requirements.

Finally, it should be also noted, that the packet loss simulation results did not reach stable values. This high variability between different executions of the same scenario may be due to the random positions of trains in the cells. Our current work concentrates on improving these results by considering fixed positions of the trains in relation to cell edges. This would reduce the variability between different executions of the same scenario.

4.3   Voice Applications (Interphone, voice announcements)

The focus in this section is put on the performance results of the voice applications (interphone and voice announcements), in relation to the number of trains at the station. Both voice applications are carried using a medium priority bearer with QCI 2 (cf. Table 2).

The recorded mean packet delay for voice applications is shown in Figure 4a. In the macro-cell deployment, the delay was between 104 ms (5 trains) and 106 ms (50 trains). In the micro-cell deployment, the delay was slightly larger: between 106 ms (5 trains) and 109 ms (50 trains). For both deployments, the delays were below the delay boundary of 150 ms required by voice applications.

The packet loss rate, in relation to the number of trains at the station, is shown in Figure 4b. In the macro-cell deployment, the packet loss rate was around 1%. It is approximately equal to the maximum packet loss required by voice applications. In the micro-cell deployment, the more trains were present at the station, the higher the packet loss was. In the case with only 5 trains at the station the packet loss was 0.14%. It increased to 1.49% with 50 trains. Thus, the packet loss in the micro-cell deployment fulfilled the requirement, only in the cases with less than 30 trains at the station. Similarly as for ETCS, the packet loss values did not converge yet to stable values.

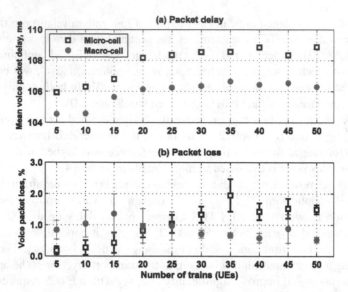

Fig. 4. Mean packet delay and packet loss ratio (with 95% confidence intervals) for voice applications in relation to the number of trains

This slightly worse performance of the micro-cell deployment was a result of the dense cell deployment. As a consequence, many trains (UEs) happened to be located at or close to an edge between two cells. The probability of packet transmission failure at a cell edge was larger than in the area close to an eNodeB. This is because, the bigger the distance to eNodeB is, the higher the interference from the neighboring cells is. As a consequence, SINR decreases and the error probability increases.

4.4   Video Surveillance Application

This subsection is focused on the communication performances experienced by the video surveillance application, which is classified as a best-effort application with QCI 9 (cf. Table 2).

In the macro-cell deployment, the video packet delay grew rapidly as shown in Figure 5a. With 15 trains, the mean delay was 180 ms. Thus, it exceeded the maximum delay required by the application, which is 100 ms (cf. Table 2). In the micro-cell deployment, the packet delay grew significantly slower. This was a result of the higher throuhput offered by the micro-cell deployment. It meant that video packets were not delayed while waiting for available tranmission resources. The packet delay exceeded the maximum allowed only in the cases with 30 trains.

In both deployments, the video packet loss grew with the number of trains in the area, as illustrated in Figure 5b. The maximum packet loss of 1% allowed by the requirements was exceeded in almost all the cases.

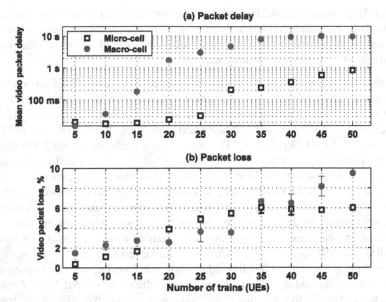

Fig. 5. Traffic throughput, mean packet delay and packet loss rate (with 95% confidence intervals) in relation to the number of trains (UEs) at the station for video surveillance application

4.5   Discussion of the Results

Let us now look, globally, at the performance offered by the two deployments.

Regarding the performance offered to the safety-critical ETCS application, both deployments offer delay performance significantly better than required by railways. However, neither of the deployments respects the packet loss ratio boundary.

For the considered voice applications, both deployments fulfill the delay and the packet loss until a load of 25 trains. The proposed micro-cell deployment is not able to ensure acceptable packet loss performance for voice in cases with more than 25 trains.

For the video surveillance application, the proposed micro-cell deployment fulfills the delay requirement until a load of 25 trains, whereas the macro-cell deployment does it only for no more than 10 trains. Regarding video packet loss ratio, both deployments violate the required boundary.

The micro-cell deployment offers significantly higher throughput, which improves the performance of the bandwidth-demanding application: the video surveillance. However, the capacity increase does not solve the issue of packet loss. In some cases (mainly for voice applications), the micro-cell deployment even increased the packet-loss ratio. This is because of the inter-cell interference, which increases error rate probability at the radio link. In the micro-cell deployment UEs have higher probability of being at a cell edge, where the interference is most severe.

Further Improvements. Additional solutions are required in order to take advantage of a micro-cell deployment without suffering from the mentioned packet loss problem discussed in the previous section. These solutions, which are to address the packet loss threshold violation, are for instance:

— Transport layer, end-to-end, retransmission mechanism for ETCS (cf. section 4.2).
— Reconfiguration of the LTE radio link retransmission mechanisms. LTE includes two retransmission mechanisms: *Hybrid Automatic Repeat reQuest (HARQ)* at the *Medium Access Control (MAC)* layer and *Automatic Repeat reQuest (ARQ)* at the *Radio Link Layer (RLC)* [16]. The packet loss performance of LTE depends on these mechanisms. For example, by increasing the maximum number of retransmissions it is possible to lower the packet loss (at the expense of increasing the packet delay). Moreover, ARQ at RLC can differentiate between EPS bearers. Thus, applications with specific packet loss requirements can be carried in an acknowledged mode to reduce the packet loss, while other less sensitive applications can be carried in an unacknowledged mode. All in all, by configuring HARQ and ARQ properly the packet loss can be reduced.
— Reconfiguration of the LTE link adaptation mechanism, which chooses the radio modulation and coding scheme depending on the observed *Bit Error Ratio (BER)*. The target for the link adaptation mechanism is to receive 90% of the transmitted packets correctly in the first transmission attempt. This results in high utilization of the radio link and a high overall throughput [7]. However, in a railway LTE network, robustness is more important than capacity due to safety concerns. Thus the link adaptation target should be increased, e.g. to receive 95% or 99% of packets correctly in the first attempt. This can be done by choosing more robust modulation and coding schemes. This would reduce the packet error probability, at the expense of reducing radio capacity. It should be also considered whether the LTE network could not take into account QoS requirements of an application, when choosing the modulation scheme.
— Adaptive video coding for video surveillance, which could reduce its data rate when the video transmission performance drops.
— Reduction of the number of simultaneous video streams transmitted in the network. By lowering the offered traffic it should be possible to avoid congestion and reduce the inter-cell interference.

5   Conclusions

LTE may become an element of future railway communication networks. This may solve railway communication-related problems and open the way for new possibilities. LTE supports new railway applications, such as video surveillance and file update. However, these new applications are very demanding in terms of throughput. Thus, railway radio access networks must be redesigned, especially in high-density railway areas, e.g. major train stations.

In this paper, an LTE micro-cell based deployment for Copenhagen Main Train Station has been presented and compared to a macro-cell based deployment. Simulation results have shown the capacity improvements of the micro-cell deployment and its positive impact on ETCS transfer delay. Moreover, a significant improvement in video throughput and video packet delay has been observed. Nevertheless, further work is required, since micro-cell deployments increase inter-cell interference. As a consequence, the packet loss increases above the values acceptable for railways. Thus, the significant packet loss becomes the greatest challenge for LTE as a likely railway communication technology.

Acknowledgment. This paper is supported by the Danish Council for Strategic Research through the RobustRailS project, the French National Fund for the digital society program through the SYSTUF project and the Institut Francais in Denmark through the Science 2013 Programme.

References

1. Winter, P., et al.: Compendium on ERTMS. Eurail Press (2009)
2. UIC, ERTMS Atlas 2012. 10th UIC ERTMS World Conference in Stockholm (2012)
3. Fisher, D.G.: Requirements on the GSM-R Network for ETCS Support. Banedanmark (2008)
4. Sniady, A., Soler, J.: An overview of GSM-R technology and its shortcomings. In: Proceedings of the 12th International Conference on ITST. IEEE (2012)
5. DTU, RobustRailS project, http://www.robustrails.man.dtu.dk
6. IFSTTAR, SYSTUF project, http://systuf.ifsttar.fr
7. Sauter, M.: From GSM to LTE: an introduction to mobile networks and mobile broadband. John Wiley and Sons, Ltd. (2011)
8. Yanase, N.: Necessities for future high speed rolling stock. International Union of Railways, UIC (2010)
9. Sniady, A., Soler, J.: Performance of LTE in High Speed Railway Scenarios. In: Berbineau, M., et al. (eds.) Nets4Cars/Nets4Trains 2013. LNCS, vol. 7865, pp. 211–222. Springer, Heidelberg (2013)
10. Sniady, A., Soler, J.: Impact of the traffic load on performance of an alternative LTE railway communication network. In: Proceedings of the 13th International Conference on ITST. IEEE (2013)
11. Khayat, A., Kassab, M., Berbineau, M., Amine Abid, M., Belghith, A.: LTE Based Communication System for Urban Guided-Transport: A QoS Performance Study. In: Berbineau, M., et al. (eds.) Nets4Cars/Nets4Trains 2013. LNCS, vol. 7865, pp. 197–210. Springer, Heidelberg (2013)
12. OPNET Modeler v.17.5 PL5, http://www.opnet.com
13. ITU-T, Recommendation G.114. One-way transmission time: International telephone connections and circuits – General Recommendations on the transmission quality for an entire international telephone connection. ITU (1996)
14. Salo, J., Nur-Alam, M., Chang, K.: Practical Introduction tp LTE Radio Planning. White Paper, European Communications Engineering (ECE) Ltd., Finland (2010)
15. OpenStreetMap, http://www.openstreetmap.org
16. ITU-R, Report ITU-R M.2135-1. Guidelines for evaluation of radio interface technologies for IMT-Advanced. ITU (2009)
17. Sesia, S., Toufik, I., Baker, M.: LTE – The UMTS Long Term Evolution From Theory to Practice. John Wiley and Sons, Ltd. (2011)
18. 3GPP, 3rd Generation Partnership Project; TS 23.203; Technical Specification Group Services and System Aspects; Policy and charging control architecture (Release 8), V8.14.0 (2012)

Live Video Streaming in Vehicular Networks

Alexey Vinel[1], Evgeny Belyaev[2], Boris Bellalta[3], and Honglin Hu[4]

[1] Halmstad University, Sweden
[2] Tampere University of Technology, Finland
[3] Universitat Pompeu Fabra, Spain
[4] Shanghai Research Center for Wireless Communications, China

Abstract. The coming years will see the adoption of IEEE 802.11p equipment, which enables broadband vehicle-to-vehicle and vehicle-to-roadside connectivity. The design and validation of prospective safety and infotainment applications in VANETs (Vehicular Ad-hoc NETworks) are currently areas of dynamic research. In this paper we introduce novel vehicular applications that are based on video transmission and targeted at improving road safety, efficiency and public security. We argue the case for the practical feasibility of the proposed applications in terms of the number of vehicles that can be supported with acceptable visual quality in VANETs environment.

Keywords: Mobile video, road safety, public security, VANET, 802.11p, WAVE.

1 Introduction

Recently approved IEEE 802.11p and IEEE 1609.4 WAVE (Wireless Access in Vehicular Environments) standards enable broadband connectivity of moving vehicles in vehicle ad-hoc NETworks (VANETs). These protocols enable the design of a wide variety of novel infotainment and road safety applications, some of which can be based on multimedia content delivery [1] – [3].

Much of the current research is dedicated to the delivery of video content, such as TV programs, from the infrastructure network to the vehicles. The key feature of these applications is that one roadside station broadcasts video streams to many vehicles. In such a case, the losses of video packets are due mainly to radio propagation-induced fading as well as the external noise in the communication channel. Nevertheless, the probability of packet losses caused by such factors can be reduced by means of the well-known techniques of Forward Error Correction (FEC) combined with Automatic repeat reQuest (ARQ) [4]. Additionally, intermediate vehicles having better link quality with the infrastructure network can be used to assist the delivery of the data packets to the destination vehicle [5] – [8].

This paper introduces a second class of video-based applications in VANETs, where the video camera is installed on the vehicle and captures the video information to be transmitted, either to other vehicles or to the infrastructure.

A. Sikora et al. (Eds.): Nets4Cars/Nets4Trains/Nets4Aircraft 2014, LNCS 8435, pp. 156–162, 2014.

Taking into account that the typical communication range of 802.11p/WAVE transceiver does not exceed 1 km, in the scenario under consideration many closely located vehicles simultaneously transmit video to the roadside unit as well as to each other. Thus, the key technical challenge of these applications is that each vehicle should estimate precisely the available random multiple access channel throughput in order to choose the video bit rate accordingly and, therefore, avoid video packet drops or transmitter buffer overflow.

The paper is organized as follows. In Section 2 we introduce examples of prospective applications in which video data is captured at the vehicle side and we show how these applications can contribute to the improvement of public security, road safety and traffic control. Section 3 presents our proposals for the robust video content delivery in such a class of applications as well as the tradeoffs between the number of vehicles and archived video quality. Section 4 contains a summary of our conclusions.

2 Examples of Applications

The video-based vehicular system being considered includes the following main components: IEEE 802.11p/WAVE transceiver, video compressing device and cameras. With this set of equipment and depending on the target area of the cameras, i.e. inside or outside the vehicle, the following applications can be implemented to improve public security, road safety and traffic control:

- overtaking assistance;
- in-vehicle video surveillance;
- traffic conditions video surveillance.

Below we describe these proposed applications in greater details.

2.1 Improving Road Safety: Overtaking Assistance

In the overtaking assistance application, a video stream captured by a windshield-mounted camera in a vehicle is compressed, broadcast to the vehicle driving behind it, and displayed to its driver. Such a "see-through" system is aimed at helping drivers overtake long and vision-obstructing vehicles, such as trucks on rural roads using the oncoming lane. Moreover, dangerous road situations or even rear-end collisions can be avoided when information about the obstacle is provided to the driver well in advance, following observation from the vision-obstructing vehicle [9], [10].

2.2 Improving Public Security: In-vehicle Video Surveillance

The in-vehicle video surveillance application captures video data by means of an internal cabin-mounted camera in a vehicle. After compression, this information is transmitted to the emergency security services such as the police and ambulance. The application will allow real-time monitoring of public transportation to help counteract terrorism, vandalism and other crimes. The efficiency of in-vehicle video surveillance can be enhanced by means of video data analysis and the detection of ctiminal activity using the state-of-the-art video analytics methods [11].

2.3 Traffic Control: Traffic Conditions Video Surveillance

For traffic control purposes it might be necessary to ascertain the current situation at a given road section, intersection or even lane. Thanks to the benefits of global positioning systems, traffic management center can activate the external cameras of vehicles located in the geographical area of interest. Video information with the current road views is then compressed at the vehicle side and transmitted back to the management center. Real-time reaction to traffic jams caused by accidents can be achieved if the video surveillance system of traffic conditions is combined with the eCall [12] or a similar system, which automatically notifies the emergency services of the crash.

3 Performance Evaluation

In future practical scenarios there are likely to be numerous closely located vehicles executing one or several of the above applications, which transmit video over the IEEE 802.11/WAVE service channels. The required video bit rate at each vehicle can be achieved by varying the video compression parameters, that define the trade-off between the visual quality and compression ratio. In order to minimize the video packet drops, the selected video bit rate of a vehicle should be consistent with the multiple access channel throughput.

One way to solve the above problem was introduced in our paper [10], where we propose that each vehicle selects its video bit rate in such a way that the service channel resources are allocated equally among all the neighboring transmitting vehicles. The key factor in this approach is proper estimation of channel throughput, that can be allocated to one vehicle, depending on the number of other transmitting vehicles in the system.

The following is the simplest estimate of the IEEE 802.11/WAVE service channel throughput per user:

$$\hat{S}_{SCH}(N) = \frac{\mu_{SCH} \cdot R}{N}, \tag{1}$$

where μ_{SCH} is the percentage of time allocated to the service channel in the control/service channels alternating scheme [2], R is the service channel data rate and N is the number of neighboring vehicles simultaneously transmitting video information on the service channel, estimated on the basis of the information from cooperative awareness messages broadcast frequently on the control channel [3].

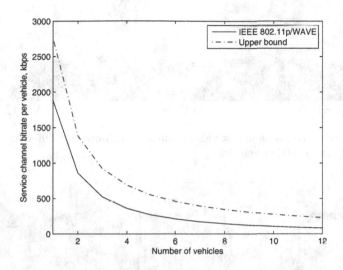

Fig. 1. IEEE 802.11p/WAVE service channel throughput per vehicle

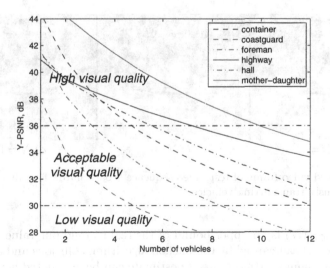

Fig. 2. Visual quality per vehicle

a) N = 1   *b) N = 6*   *c) N = 12*

Fig. 3. Received video frame of test video sequence "highway" for different number of simultaneously transmitting vehicles

a) N = 1   *b) N = 6*   *c) N = 12*

Fig. 4. Received video frame of test video sequence "hall" for different number of simultaneously transmitting vehicles

a) N = 1   *b) N = 6*   *c) N = 12*

Fig. 5. Received video frame of test video sequence "coastguard" for different number of simultaneously transmitting vehicles

In fact, $\hat{S}_{SCH}(N)$ is an upper bound of the real throughput value, because it neglects the overhead caused by the backoff algorithm, collisions and availability of the service channel. A more precise estimate can be calculated as:

$$S_{SCH}(N) = \frac{\mu_{SCH} \cdot \rho(N) \cdot S_{802.11}(N) \cdot R}{N}, \tag{2}$$

where $\rho(N)$ is the probability of service channel availability due to the successful reception of the corresponding wireless service advertisement [16], $S_{802.11}(N)$ is the throughput of legacy 802.11 basic access scheme with N saturated stations.

The values of S_{SCH} for $R = 6$ Mbit/s, $\mu_{SCH} = 0.46$ [2] and the different number of transmitting vehicles N are shown in Fig. 1. On the basis of these data we demonstrate the corresponding maximum achievable visual quality, as shown in Fig. 2. For visual quality measurements we use x.264 codec [13], which is the real-time software implementation of the H.264/AVC standard [14]. The test video sequences "container", "coastguard", "foreman", "highway", "hall", "mother-daughter" [15] with a frame resolution 352×288, 30 frames per second were used. These sequences correspond to typical scenarios for the considered applications, e.g. indoor video surveillance with high or low level of objects mobility, view from the moving vehicle, etc.

The well-known peak signal-to-noise ratio (PSNR) was used as a visual quality metric. Typically, PSNR greater than 36 dB corresponds to high visual quality (received video either cannot be distinguished visually from the captured one). PSNR less than 30 dB corresponds to low visual quality (received video contains a lot of distortions). PSNR from 30 to 36 dB corresponds to acceptable visual quality. For video quality estimation each test video sequence is compressed by x.264 encoder for given bit rate per user. Then video stream is decompressed and PSNR values between original and reconstructed video sequences are computed.

From Fig. 2, it follows that high and acceptable video quality can be achieved if the number of closely located vehicles broadcasting video simultaneously on a selected service channel does not exceed 5–12 in most of the cases. Taking into account that six service channels are available, according to [2], the above maximum number of vehicles can be increased up to 40–70 depending on application. Examples of received video frame of test video sequences for different number of simultaneously transmitting vehicles are given at Fig. 3–5.

4 Conclusion

We have introduced novel video-based vehicular applications that promote road safety and public security as well as the efficiency of road traffic control. The key feature of the proposed applications is that many moving vehicles perform video transmission to each other and to the roadside infrastructure. We have demonstrated that the emergent IEEE 802.11p/WAVE standard can serve as a basis of communication for the above applications, given that video bit rate is chosen in accordance with the available throughput of the service channels used. Our analysis shows that 40–70 vehicles in the vicinity can be served simultaneously with acceptable visual quality, which in our view confirms the practical feasibility of the proposed approach.

References

1. IEEE 802.11p, Wireless Access in Vehicular Environments (July 2010)
2. IEEE 1609.4-2010, IEEE Standard for Wireless Access in Vehicular Environments (WAVE) - Multi-channel Operation (February 2011)
3. Karagiannis, G., Altintas, O., Ekici, E., Heijenk, G.J., Jarupan, B., Lin, K., Weil, T.: Vehicular networking: A survey and tutorial on requirements, architectures, challenges, standards and solutions. IEEE Communications Surveys and Tutorials 13(4), 584–616 (2011)
4. Tsai, M.F., Chilamkurti, N., Zeadally, S., Vinel, A.: Concurrent multipath transmission combining forward error correction and path interleaving for video streaming. Computer Communications 34(9), 1125–1136 (2011)
5. Qadri, N.N., Fleury, M., Altaf, M., Ghanbari, M.: Multi-source video streaming in a wireless vehicular ad hoc network. IET Communications 4(11), 1300–1311 (2010)
6. Asefi, M., Mark, J.W., Shen, X.: An Application-Centric Inter-Vehicle Routing Protocol for Video Streaming over Multi-Hop Urban VANETs. In: IEEE International Conference on Communications (ICC 2011), Kyoto (June 2011)
7. Zhou, L., Zhang, Y., Song, K., Jing, W., Vasilakos, A.: Distributed Media Services in P2P-Based Vehicular Networks. IEEE Transactions on Vehicular Technology 60(2), 692–703 (2011)
8. Soldo, F., Casetti, C., Chiasserini, C.-F., Chaparro, P.A.: Video Streaming Distribution in VANETs. IEEE Transactions on Parallel and Distributed Systems 22(7), 1085–1091 (2011)
9. Gomes, P., Olaverri-Monreal, C., Ferreira, M.: Making Vehicles Transparent through V2V Video Streaming. IEEE Transactions on Intelligent Transportation Systems 13(2), 930–938 (2012)
10. Vinel, A., Belyaev, E., Egiazarian, K., Koucheryavy, Y.: An overtaking assistance system based on joint beaconing and real-time video transmission. IEEE Transactions on Vehicular Technology 61(5), 2319–2329 (2012)
11. Liu, H., Chen, S., Kubota, N.: Special Section on Intelligent Video Systems and Analytics. IEEE Transactions on Industrial Informatics 8(1) (2012)
12. eCall: http://ec.europa.eu/information_society/activities/esafety/ecall/index_en.htm
13. x.264 video codec: http://x264.nl/
14. Advanced video coding for generic audiovisual services, ITU-T Recommendation H.264 and ISO/IEC 14496-10, AVC (2009)
15. Xiph.org test media: http://media.xiph.org/video/derf/
16. Campolo, C., Molinaro, A., Vinel, A., Zhang, Y.: Modeling Prioritized Broadcasting in Multichannel Vehicular Networks. IEEE Transactions on Vehicular Technology 61(2), 687–701 (2012)

Author Index

Bellalta, Boris   156
Belyaev, Evgeny   156
Berbineau, Marion   143
Binhack, Michael   23
Bittl, Sebastian   113
Böhm, Annette   30
Breu, Jakob   43

Chibelushi, Claude C.   57

Fischer, Wolfgang   69
Fröhlich, Johannes   94

Garcia, Fabien   81
Geyer, Fabien   69

Hakobyan, Gor   57
Hämäläinen, Matti   1
Hu, Honglin   156

Iinatti, Jari   1

Jonsson, Magnus   30

Kassab, Mohamed   143
Kuehbeck, Thomas   57

Kunert, Kristina   30
Kupris, Gerald   23

Mayer, Erwin   94
Menth, Michael   43
Möllendorf, Lars   11
Moniri, Mansour   57

Pirovano, Alain   81

Radzik, José   81
Rahman, Md. Arafatur   103

Schappacher, Manuel   11
Schneele, Stefan   69
Sekiguchi, Tatsuya   126
Sikora, Axel   11, 57
Sniady, Aleksander   143
Soderi, Simone   1
Soler, José   143

Tsuboi, Tsutomu   126

Vey, Quentin   81
Viittala, Harri   1
Vinel, Alexey   30, 156